Gillo Pontecorvo

From Resistance to Terrorism

Carlo Celli

THE SCARECROW PRESS, INC.

Lanham, Maryland · Toronto · Oxford

2005

SCARECROW PRESS, INC.

Published in the United States of America
by Scarecrow Press, Inc.
A wholly owned subsidary of
The Rowman & Littlefield Publishing Group, Inc.
4501 Forbes Boulevard, Suite 200, Lanham, Maryland 20706
www.scarecrowpress.com

PO Box 317
Oxford
OX2 9RU, UK

British Library Cataloguing in Publication Information Available

Library of Congress Cataloging-in-Publication Data

Celli, Carlo, 1963–
  Gillo Pontecorvo : from resistance to terrorism / Carlo Celli.
    p. cm.
  Filmography: p.
  Includes bibliographical references and index.
  ISBN 0-8108-5440-6 (pbk. : alk. paper)
  1. Pontecorvo, Gillo, 1919– I. Title.

PN1998.3.P664C45 2005
791.4302'33'092—dc22

                                              2005009705

⊚™ The paper used in this publication meets the minimum requirements of
American National Standard for Information Sciences—Permanence of Paper
for Printed Library Materials, ANSI/NISO Z39.48-1992.
Manufactured in the United States of America

Contents

Preface

Gillo Pontecorvo directing Burn! *Courtesy of Photofest*

$\mathscr{A}$s Gillo Pontecorvo's films have aged and the the events they depict have faded into history, his work deserves to be reexamined. His masterpiece, *La battaglia di Algeri/The Battle of Algiers* (1966), has attained new relevance due to the rise of Islamic terrorism. Pontecorvo was intricately involved in many of the key moments of the second half of the twentieth century. He was an assimilated Italian Jew active in the anti-Nazi/Fascist resistance in World War II. He was an important figure of the independent Left of the Euro-communist period following his departure from the Italian Communist Party (PCI) after the Soviet Union's repression of a prodemocracy revolt in Hungary in 1956. Pontecorvo made only five feature films between 1957 and 1979. Yet his films examine key cultural and political issues: women's rights in *Giovanna* (1956), worker solidarity in *La grande strada azzurra/The Wide Blue Road* (1957), the Holocaust in *Kapò* (1960), national liberation struggles in *The Battle of Algiers* (1966), colonialism and postcolonialism in *Queimada!/Burn!* (1969), and terrorism within the context of nascent republican institutions in *Operation Ogre/Ogro* (1979).

Pontecorvo's service as a leader in the anti-Nazi/Fascist resistance of World War II Italy—with its clandestine armed struggle, popular strikes, and uprisings—and his introduction to the methods of Italian neorealism as an actor and assistant director on Aldo Vergano's World War II resistance drama *Il sole sorge ancora/Outcry* (1946) were the foundation of his subsequent cinematic work. The ideal of a common struggle against oppression was a theme in many films of the Italian neorealist period after World War II, including those that had a direct influence on Pontecorvo, such as Roberto Rossellini's *Paisan/Paisà* (1946). Pontecorvo's first films, *Giovanna* (1956) and *The Wide Blue Road* (1957), were made well after the height of Italian neorealist production in the late 1940s. Yet Pontecorvo's first features reflect the ideological moment of Italian neorealism with narratives that contrast collective responsibilities with individual impulse. Pontecorvo retained this narrative of colletivism versus individualism in his later films, adding a current of historical determinism by interpreting individual action as secondary to the historical progressions in Marxist precepts. In accordance with this deterministic vision of history, Pontecorvo's films portray the individual as an agent of larger forces that mold the course of his or her free will.

When Pontecorvo sought to transpose the model of national liberation struggles of his experience in the anti-Nazi/Fascist resistance to other historical settings, the resulting films reveal some limitations in his ideological conditioning. If Pontecorvo's film *Kapò* is read within the historical context of anti-Semitism in Europe, the film reveals unsettling narrative similarities with previous Jewish representation in Italian film and European literature in which Jewish characters are eliminated after displaying the sort of negative character traits that are staples of centuries-old anti-Semitic propaganda. The reduction of the story of a Jewish Parisian girl deported to a Nazi camp in *Kapò* to an allegory about individual versus collective ideals underemphasizes the importance of the racist grounding of Nazi ideology within the context of European history.

Due to the recent rise of Islamic terrorism, *The Battle of Algiers* is no longer a film whose relevance is limited to the period of anticolonial struggles of the 1960s. The film has, in fact, been adopted by the political Right and the Left as a training tool by both terrorist and antiterrorist groups.[1] A possible explanation for the enduring popularity of *The Battle of Algiers* among both insurgent and anti-insurgent groups may be that the film actually has two endings. One ending highlights the success of the French paratroopers' campaign against the rebellion in the city of Algiers in the late 1950s. The other ending is a coda depicting popular, spontaneous uprisings in Algiers in the early 1960s, which led to the ultimate achievement of Algerian independence from France. With this coda Pontecorvo hoped to communicate how the attacks and general strikes organized by the Algerian independence movement of the Algerian National Liberation Front (FLN) successfully created a sense of national consciousness among the Algerian populace, a point in common with Pontecorvo's own experiences in the Italian resistance during World War II. Particularly in consideration of the film's current popularity on both the political Left and Right, the two endings and matter-of-fact depiction of the use of violence and torture by French anti-insurgents and Algerian insurgents impart a more basic and troubling message—that violence is the key method by which political forces seek to establish and retain legitimacy.

If Pontecorvo's most lauded films—*Kapò* and *The Battle of Algiers*, both nominated for Academy Awards—display unintended narrative currents about Jewish representation or the rationalization of violence, Pontecorvo's ideological preconceptions served him better in his most undervalued film, *Burn!* (1969). The film is a Pygmalion-like allegory about the process of colonialism and postcolonialism featuring a brilliant performance by Marlon Brando as an individual who is a conscious motor of history. *Burn!* has a circular narrative that depicts successive revolts by an indigenous population that are defeated by an island's status quo and international powers.[2] The depiction of a fictional Caribbean island nation in *Burn!* makes it one of few widely distributed films that provide an account of the transition from traditional colonialism to corporate-based postcolonialism. Thus *Burn!* is a film with vast resonance not only for the experiences of former colonies in Africa and South America but for any country burdened with legacies of human slavery and racism.

Pontecorvo's last feature, *Ogro* (1979), is perhaps the key film in his opus. *Ogro* was planned as a straight, chronological depiction of the Basque *Euzkadi Ta Askatasuna* (ETA) terrorist assassination of Franchist minister Carrero Blanco in 1973 Spain. But Pontecorvo felt obligated to change the narrative of the film to question terrorism after the kidnapping and murder of former Italian premier Aldo Moro by communist terrorists in 1978. Pontecorvo has admitted that *Ogro* was actually made with a guilty conscience due to concurrent events in Italy.[3] He attempted to salvage the film by including characterizations that question the legitimacy of terrorism. But these additions make *Ogro* a film that contradicts itself. The film's heroic depiction of a terrorist act is enveloped by flashbacks and a coda in which a Basque ETA terrorist on his hospital deathbed admits his fears about meeting his maker in light of the violent life he led. His comrades attempt to comfort him by praising his courage to act on his convictions. But in the final scenes they distance themselves from their hard-line comrade's belief in violence as a legitimate political tool. The scene is a fitting finale for Pontecorvo's entire opus, which runs from the enthusiasm of his appearance as a resistance fighter in *Outcry*, to his vivid depiction of armed struggle in *The Battle of Algiers*, to the fatalism of *Burn!*, and finally the retreat from terrorism with the guilty conscience of *Ogro*.

Perhaps the key questions in an examination of Pontecorvo are why he made so few films (five features) and, more importantly, why he did not complete a feature film after *Ogro* in 1979. Pontecorvo was physically vibrant enough to accept postings in Italian cultural institutions as head of the Venice film festival and the Cinecittà studios in Rome in the 1990s. In interviews Pontecorvo has explained his lack of artistic productivity since *Ogro* not as an ideological retreat, but as a sort of character flaw.[4] Pontecorvo has insisted that after *Ogro* he was stubbornly unable to commit to a feature film project unless he was absolutely convinced of its necessity. If this is the case, interpretation of Pontecorvo's life and work could cast him as a disillusioned purist or, based on his statements in a late interview, as a Crocean idealist, who finds that the world has not lived up to his expectations and as a result decides to retreat into a shell of creative inactivity.[5] However, Pontecorvo's explanations about his artistic denouement are contradicted by the content of two important films he did complete after *Ogro*: a documentary, *Ritorno ad Algeri/Return to Algiers* (1992); and a short, *Protection Nostalgia* (1997). *Return to Algiers* (1992) is a little-known documentary made for Italian state television that chronicles Pontecorvo's return to the site of his masterpiece, *The Battle of Algiers* (1966), to witness that country's 1991 struggle with Islamic fundamentalism and civil conflict. Pontecorvo's *Nostalgia di protezione/Protection Nostalgia* (1997) is a short film about a Roman businessman who dreams longingly for the innocence of boyhood under the protective wing of his mother. *Protection Nostalgia*, in particular, was not well received at the few film festivals where it was screened. Audiences simply did not expect a film with themes of personal withdrawal and nostalgia from Pontecorvo. Despite his lack of film production over the latest period of his life, Pontecorvo retained a reputation as a figure committed to the ideological message of armed struggle of his earlier features.

Yet like the last scenes of *Ogro*, in which characters distance themselves from their earlier commitment to terrorism, Pontecorvo's last films, *Protection Nostalgia* and *Return to Algiers*, serve as a coda to the films of his earlier career.

Unfortunately, Pontecorvo never made his last great film project, *Il tempo della fine/The Time of the End*, about the life of Jesus. The film, which is actually only one of many uncompleted projects, might have allowed Pontecorvo an opportunity to resolve the contradiction of themes of justification of violence and terrorism for reasons of national liberation, in this case the struggle of the Jews for liberation from the Roman Empire, in the historical setting of the birth of Christianity, a religion whose ethical core condemns violence.[6] Perhaps Pontecorvo's last two documentaries should be read in consideration of the themes that he could have resolved in a film about Jesus in the midst of an anti-Roman rebellion. The fact that Pontecorvo distanced himself from the ideological certainty of his first features (*Kapò, The Battle of Algiers*) in *Ogro* and his last documentaries (*Protection Nostalgia* and *Return to Algiers*) could be interpreted as an expression of maturity. To see the elderly Pontecorvo conducting interviews in an Algeria on the brink of de facto civil war in his 1992 documentary *Return to Algiers* is to realize how complicated political issues have become since Pontecorvo's foundational experiences in the clear-cut, good-versus-evil struggle against Nazism/Fascism in the Italian resistance. Pontecorvo's career, from his first appearance as an actor in the neorealist resistance drama *Outcry* (1946) to his last short, *Protection Nostalgia*, is emblematic of the ideological pitfalls of the twentieth century in all of its hopes and contradictions.[7]

NOTES

1. See Stuart Klawans, "Lessons of the Pentagon's Favorite Training Film," *New York Times*, January 4, 2004, 26.

2. See Carlo Celli, "A Master Narrative in Italian Cinema?" *Italica* 81, no. 1 (2004): 73–83.

3. "Intervista a Gillo Pontecorvo," *Ogro*, DVD (Rome: Cristaldi Film, 2003).

4. Irene Bignardi, *Memorie estorte a uno smemeorato vita di Gillo Pontecorvo* (Milan: Feltrinelli, 1999, 173.

5. Bignardi, *Memorie*, 159.

6. Francesco Bolzoni, "Un film su Gesù Conversazione di Gillo Pontecorvo con Francesco Bolzoni," in *Primo piano sull'autore Gillo Pontecorvo "La dittatura della verità,"* ed. Luigi Cipriani, M. Conciatori, M. Giraldi, and L. Ricci (Rome: Designer, 1999), 133–39.

7. Carlo Celli, "Gillo Pontecorvo's *Return to Algiers* (1992)," *Film Quarterly* 58, no. 2 (2004), 49–52.

Acknowledgments

$\mathscr{I}$ would like to thank Stephen Ryan, Nicole McCullough, and Bevin McLaughlin at Scarecrow Press; Sergio Toffetti and Flavia Morabito of the archives of the Scuola Nazionale di Cinema Rome; Cinzia Pistolesi and Sandra Eichberg of the RAI Direzione Teche e Servizi Tematici/Educativi; Gianluca Farinelli, Anna Fiaccarini, Enrica Serrani, and Cesare Ballardini of the Cineteca del Comune di Bologna; Silvia Bruni and Salvatore Scali at the Biblioteca Rai in Rome; the Archivio Audiovisivo del Moviemento Operaio e Democratico in Rome; Antonio Breschi of Cinecittà Holding in Rome; Maddalena Bianchi of Movietime Italian Films distribution for providing a study copy of *The Wide Blue Road*; Dennis Doros of Milestone Films for allowing still reprints from *The Wide Blue Road*. An earlier version of a section of chapter 1 appeared as an article in *Forum Italicum* as "Aldo Vergano's *Il sole sorge ancora/Outcry* (1946) as Influence on Gillo Pontecorvo," *Forum Italicum* 38, no. 1 (Spring 2004): 217–28. My thanks to editor Mario Mignone for allowing a reprint. A shortened version of a portion of chapter 8 appeared in *Film Quarterly* as "Gillo Pontecorvo's *Return to Algiers*" (1992), *Film Quarterly* 58, no. 2 (2004): 49–52. My thanks to University of California Press editor Anne Martin, guest editor Catherine Zimmer, and subsidiary rights manager Darcy J. Dapra. Photos on pages v, 49, 51, 72, 73, 77, 82, 84, and 89 and copyright permissions are courtesy of Photofest.

Above all, I would like to thank my wife, Larissa, and my children, Marco and Sofia, for providing what is most important in life.

Introduction

$\mathcal{G}$illo Pontecorvo was born in Pisa in 1919, the fifth of eight children. His position as the eldest of the youngest children had a self-admitted influence on the formation of his stubborn but also self-doubting character. The next eldest in the family was nearly seven years his senior. The head of the Pontecorvo family, Massimo, was an assimilated Jew who owned a textile factory. At the height of its activity the factory reportedly employed hundreds of workers. The Pontecorvo family was quite wealthy until a crisis in the textile industry reduced family fortunes.[1]

Pontecorvo's education was typical for someone of his class. His parents employed a live-in French nanny to teach their children French. A musical education was encouraged for the children, especially the daughters. Pontecorvo's father reportedly would gather his children to perform improvised concerts in which parts were hummed rather than performed on instruments. This composing technique remained with Pontecorvo, who never had any formal musical training. The exposure to music would become an important element in Pontecorvo's career as a director; he made contributions to the sound tracks of his early documentaries and his later features, including *Kapò* (1959) and *La battaglia di Algeri/The Battle of Algiers* (1966). Pontecorvo has even declared in later interviews his regret at not becoming a composer or orchestra conductor instead of a film director.[2] Due to family pressure, Pontecorvo did not study music, as males were expected to receive a more technical training. Gillo's eldest brother, Guido, became a genetic scientist; another brother became a research engineer. Most notorious among the Pontecorvo offspring was the physicist, Bruno, who worked with Enrico Fermi; Bruno defected to the Soviet Union's nuclear arms program in 1950 during the height of the Cold War.[3] Gillo has admitted a sense of inferiority with respect to these older siblings as a determining factor in the formation of his rebellious and stubborn character. In fact Gillo never performed brilliantly in school, although this was apparently not due to a lack of talent or intelligence. He was allegedly able to complete two years of high school exams in a single year, catching up with his age group in order to enter university on schedule. Family pressure drove Gillo to briefly pursue a degree in chemistry at the University of Pisa. Pontecorvo admitted that his inclination would have been to study literature, music, or the arts—fields that the family considered suitable only for female education.[4]

Pontecorvo never completed his course of university study partly because he had the good fortune to be an excellent tennis player. Success on the tennis court led to a brief tour on the European professional tennis circuit, including stops in the south of France and later in Paris, where in 1938 Gillo stayed with his brother Bruno, the physicist who would later defect to the Soviet Union.[5] Bruno Pontecorvo was living in the Paris of the idealistic moment of the Popular Front, when a progressive coalition led the French government prior to the outbreak of World War II. Through Bruno, Gillo met Italian expatriots and Italian anti-Fascist sympathizers living in Paris. Gillo's formal schooling in 1930s Italy had of course been under the control of Mussolini's Fascist regime. Thus as a young tennis professional Gillo was enthralled by the political enthusiasm among Bruno's comrades. Gillo became heavily influenced by the Marxist ideas of his older brother. Of course, when the German army began its approach to Paris, Gillo put ideology aside and fled to the south of France at St. Tropez, familiar territory from his brief tour on the professional tennis circuit. During the war the south of France remained somewhat outside the sphere of direct German occupation, and thus became a magnet for refugees from throughout Europe. With the outbreak of war Gillo, then also newly married, found himself cut off from the financial resources of his parents. He later recounted that he was able to make a meager living by giving tennis lessons to rich refugees and doing some spear fishing. During this early period of the war Pontecorvo met cultural luminaries including Tristan Tzara, the Dadaist artist, and reportedly enjoyed a crash course in music theory from the composer René Leibowitz.[6]

Due to Nazi Germany's conquest of much of continental Europe during World War II, the Pontecorvo family's Jewish origins became a cause of desperate concern, although Pontecorvo has reported that a sense of Jewish identity had never been a major part of his family life.[7] The Italian Fascist regime had made the first step toward open anti-Semitic policies in 1938 with the passage of the *leggi razziali* (racial statutes). These laws restricted the civil liberties of Jews by prohibiting, among other activities, attendance in public school, holding public jobs, marrying outside their religion, owning large tracts of land. These restrictions became increasingly severe, culminating in the deportation of Italian Jews to Auschwitz between 1943 and 1945.[8] Like many other Jews in Europe, Pontecorvo's parents had not fully realized the gravity of their predicament and were fortunate to escape to Switzerland before the end of the war.[9]

After Anglo-American forces liberated Sicily in 1943, Italy was effectively divided in half. Northern Italy remained under the control of Nazi Germany, aided by Italians loyal to Fascism, under the Republic of Salò, a puppet government headed by Mussolini at Salò, a resort town on Lake Garda. Allied armies successfully invaded Sicily in the summer of 1943. Italian king Victor Emmanuel III appointed Italian army general Pietro Badoglio as head of a provisory government after dismissing Mussolini. The Vatican began to position itself for a postwar world to defer embarrassment following the studied inaction of Pope Pius XII (1876–1958) against Nazi/Fascist policies. Following instructions from Moscow, exiled Italian communist leader Palmiro Togliatti announced the *svolta di Salerno* (the Salerno about-face), which instructed communist party members and sympathizers to cooperate with royalists and other anti-Fascist forces. These events set the stage for the loose confederation of anti-Nazi/Fascist forces—made up of Catholics, communists, and liberals—known as the resistance. Partisan resistance groups were formed around former soldiers and escaped prisoners of war hiding in the hills with the aid of the local peasantry; their insurrectionary campaign was a mixture of anti-Nazi/Fascist sabotage and settling of personal scores, as often occurs in civil conflicts. The so-called Committees of National Liberation (CLN) leading the resistance weakened Nazi control in the north and helped prepare the way for the Allied armies stalled in the mountainous Italian terrain. The resistance in Italy gained legendary status, which added significantly to the prestige of future members of the Italian Communist Party, like Pontecorvo, who were active in the resistance leadership. In March of 1944 the CLN mobilized general strikes, an event evoked in Pontecorvo's film *The Battle of Algiers*. The end of the war in Italy was characterized by popular uprisings in large cities like Milan and Genoa, so that Allied troops at times were met by victorious representatives of the CLN resistance as well as surrendering German and Fascist troops.

As mentioned, during the early war years Pontecorvo made important contacts among Italian expatriates in the south of France. By 1942 he had also become a courier between the exiled leadership of the Italian underground in the unoccupied south of France and their contacts in Italy. Pontecorvo has claimed he was approached by the Italian anti-Nazi/Fascist resistance because the Fascist regime's secret police (OVRA) apparently did not have a file on him, and he was thus able to cross the French-Italian border with comparative ease.[10] Through his contacts with Italian exiles he received further ideological education from future leaders of the postwar Italian Communist Party like Giorgio Amendola and Cesare Negarville. He also met the Italian republican leader Ugo la Malfa and other expatriates involved with anti-Fascist political organizations that would be important in the formation of the postwar republic in Italy. After a dragnet of members of the Milan resistance in 1943, Gillo went to Milan under the code name Barnaba to fill voids in the resistance organization. Pontecorvo became intricately involved in the anti-Fascist resistance in the Eugenio Curiel brigade, eventually as commander. He gained close ties to other resistance activists who would be key figures in the future leadership of the Italian Communist Party, like Pietro Ingrao and Enrico Berlinguer. Pontecorvo also worked as an underground journalist on the first issues of the clandestine communist newspaper *L'Unità*, the future official organ of the postwar Italian Communist Party. When Pontecorvo's photograph was circulated among the Fascist police in Milan, he moved to Turin to continue in the underground, organizing general strikes and clandestine resistance activity.[11]

The resistance in which Pontecorvo was an active participant would be a major factor in the political climate of postwar Italy. The efforts of the royalist government in exile, allied with partisan groups, against Nazi German troops, supported by Fascist sympathizers and draftees of the Republic of Salò (which included important postwar figures like dramatist Dario Fo) had proved that there had been an indigenous reaction against Fascism. The fact that some Italians had fought and defeated Nazism/Fascism independently helped to create a political mythology about the resistance that somewhat assuaged the feeling of collective responsibility after Italy's long submission to Fascism and the humiliating defeat of Mussolini's regime. The myth of the resistance allowed Italians to attenuate the level of war guilt felt in Germany, for example, for the atrocities committed against Jews and other ethnic groups in the Holocaust. But it is estimated that through the complicity of the Italian forces in northern Italy after September 8, 1943, approximately eighty-five hundred Italian Jews were deported to the Nazi death camp at Auschwitz.[12] Themes of clandestine living and armed struggle echoing Pontecorvo's resistance experience appear in some form in all of his feature films. The importance of the resistance experience in Pontecorvo's work cannot be underestimated. The connections and friendships that Pontecorvo made during these years of activity in the resistance among the future leaders of the Italian Communist Party would be of pivotal importance for his future career and life as a member of the left-wing elite in Italy. In fact after the war most if not all of Pontecorvo's colleagues who had been leaders of the resistance had the opportunity to enter politics and serve in the Italian constitutional assembly. Had Pontecorvo taken this path it would have a stepping-stone to a political career.

However, after the heady and tragic experiences of the war, instead of politics Pontecorvo was attracted to journalism. He had been part of the group that had published the first clandestine copies of the Communist Party paper *L'Unità* during the war. With his background as a resistance leader and connections in the world of the Italian Left, he was able to find a post at the Socialist and Communist party youth magazine *Pattuglia*, reporting directly to Italian Communist Party chief Palmiro Togliatti. In this setting Pontecorvo continued to cultivate friendships with the elite of Italian political and cultural life. It was through his experience as a journalist that Pontecorvo gained expertise in photography, although he has recounted that his interest in photography was also a means to earn extra money during the war years.[13]

Pontecorvo's first important experience in the cinema was as assistant director and actor in Aldo Vergano's World War II resistance drama *Il sole sorge ancora/Outcry* (1946), a film partly funded by an Italian ex-partisan organization. The film depicts the civil strife in northern Italy following the Italian monarchy's decision to dismiss Mussolini as premier and switch to the Allied side on September 8, 1943. The film's central theme concerns collaboration between the Italians and the Nazis/Fascists, as well as the tenuous union between Catholics and communists in the resistance. For his role as Pietro, a partisan fighter, Pontecorvo drew from his wartime experiences and appeared with other future directors Carlo Lizzani and Giuseppe De Santis.

In later interviews Pontecorvo has never emphasized the importance of his experience acting in Vergano's film. However, his role as Pietro, the martyred resistance fighter in *Outcry*, seems to have had a huge resonance on Pontecorvo's later films. In *Outcry* Pontecorvo was a nonprofessional actor who took direction from Vergano, an experienced professional in the Italian cinema industry. Vergano was part of the generation of directors who had been trained in the Italian professional cinema of the 1930s and who came out of the experience of World War II with a sense of mission to make films that were a clear departure from the rhetoric of the defeated Fascist regime. Vergano's film is a key example of the film style known as Italian neorealism, which was developed in works such as Roberto Rossellini's *Roma città aperta/Rome Open City* (1945), *Paisan/Paisà* (1946), *Germani anno zero/Germany Year Zero* (1948); Vittorio De Sica's *Sciuscià/Shoeshine* (1946) and *Ladri di biciclette/The Bicycle Thief* (1948); and Luchino Visconti's *La terra trema/The Earth Trembles* (1948). These directors worked in a style that recalled the Italian literary school of *verismo* (naturalism) and sought an objective portrayal of life with the use of nonprofessional actors, on-location shooting, and stories that featured common people in progressively tinged plots. Pontecorvo's debt to the neorealist style can be seen in his adoption, in later feature films, of a documentary style, progressively tinged narratives, on-location shooting, and above all the casting of nonprofessional actors such as Brahim Haggiag as Ali Le Pointe in *The Battle of Algiers*. The influence of Vergano's *Outcry* on Pontecorvo should not be underestimated. The plot of the film, with characters caught in personal moral dilemmas that reflect larger historical struggles, would repeat in each of Pontecorvo's features. The very plot structure of *Outcry*, which revolves around keen characterizations of the Nazi/Fascist and resistance factions and ends in a popular uprising, presages the narratives of Pontecorvo's feature films, like *The Battle of Algiers* and *Kapò*.[14]

A pivotal experience in Pontecorvo's life—as in the lives of the generation of Italian neorealist directors—was the historical moment of the anti-Nazi/Fascist resistance and the fall of the Fascist regime in Italy. But Pontecorvo was a bit younger than many of the renowned names of the neorealist tradition, including Rossellini, De Sica, and Visconti. These famed directors had been active in Italian cultural life during the *ventennio*, the nearly twenty-year period (1922–1943) of Fascist rule. Pontecorvo was born in 1919 and came to the cinema after the war. For Pontecorvo, the World War II experience in the resistance of clandestine living, armed struggle, and general strikes had been a foundational experience and not a matter of repositioning for a post-Fascist world. Pontecorvo's first-hand experiences in the war and resistance would fire the narratives of his subsequent films as a director.

After the war, Pontecorvo returned to France to work as a journalist for a French press agency (the *Agence Havas*, now *France-Presse*); in this position, he interviewed intellectuals, including existentialist philosopher Jean Paul Sartre and Spanish painter Pablo Picasso. Pontecorvo also served as a Paris correspondent for Italian newspapers such as *Repubblica* and *Paese Sera*. However, rather than the articles, what really excited Pontecorvo were the accompanying photographs. Pontecorvo brought cameras from Italy to France, where such consumer goods were scarce, and he began to gain familiarity with photographic equipment, to the point that he developed a further interest in film. As a budding photojournalist, Gillo attained the expertise in the handling of film stock and lighting that would be a fundamental aspect of the documentary style of his films. Ironically, his editors would criticize him for putting too much emphasis on the photographic elements of his reports.[15]

The incident that, according to Pontecorvo's later recounting of events, led to his career in the cinema was seeing Roberto Rossellini's neorealist war docudrama *Paisà/Paisan* (1946) while in Paris working as a journalist. The film portrays the Anglo-American liberation of Italy during World War II, with episodes depicting the Allies' slow progress up the Italian peninsula. Pontecorvo was particularly struck by the film's final episode, set in the Po valley, in which an American operative of OSS (the agency that was the forerunner of the CIA) and a group of partisans are hunted down by the Nazis/Fascists. The episode had terrible relevance to Pontecorvo's own experiences in the wartime resistance. Pontecorvo was also taken with the neorealist style of Rossellini's film, with its vivid and unaffected recreation of the wartime atmosphere. For Pontecorvo, seeing Rossellini's film was a turning point. He has claimed that he subsequently decided to abandon everything in order to work in the cinema.[16] The neorealist style of Rossellini's *Paisà* communicated the experience of the war and the resistance. It created a narrative for a postwar Italian republic based on the idealistic notion that Italy had struggled, if not autonomously, then at least honorably, through active resistance against the Nazi/Fascist shadow.[17] The success of the CLN coalition created a national desire for moral, political, and economic renewal. The myths established about the resistance served as a basis for a culture of collective understanding and reaction against fascism. For Pontecorvo this was not mere rhetoric. When he saw the resistance depicted in Rossellini's film *Paisà*, it changed his life, and he decided that his path lay in the cinema. The neorealist style and sense of mission about the themes of popular struggles and armed resistance in Rossellini's film rang true with Pontecorvo and would pervade all of his later work.

After seeing *Paisà* Pontecorvo began to seek work in the film industry as an assistant director. In France he was assistant director on a Totò Marcanton documentary and to Yves Allégret on *Les miracles n'ont lieu qu'une fois/Miracles Only Happen Once* (1951) starring Jean Marais and Alida Valli, a film about a love relationship between the French Marais (Jerome) and the Italian Valli (Claudia) interrupted by war. In Italy, Pontecorvo assisted Giancarlo Menotti on the film version of his opera *The Medium* (1951) as well as Mario Monicelli on the drama *Le infedeli/The Unfaithfuls* (1952). He also assisted Monicelli on *Totò and Carolina/Totò and Caroline*, featuring Italian comedian Totò (Antonio De Curtis), shot in 1953 and released two years later. Pontecorvo has stated that he learned a great deal of practical filmmaking techniques from the experience with Monicelli.[18]

Besides gaining experience as an assistant director, Pontecorvo made use of Italian governmental subsidies to direct documentaries in a style heavily influenced by the taste for Italian neorealism he acquired from watching Rossellini's *Paisà*. Pontecorvo was also influenced by the montage techniques and style of Ukrainian director Aleksandr Dovzhenko and Russian directors like Sergei Eisenstein and Nicolai Ekk, and in particular Ekk's film *The Road to Life* (1931), about troubled youth during the Russian revolutionary and civil wars.[19] In these early documentaries Pontecorvo adapted the stylistic tenets of Italian neorealism to subjects that were an appropriate vehicle for his progressive politics. Pontecorvo's first effort, *La Missione Timiriazev/The Timiriazev Mission* (1953), funded by Italian labor unions and Communist Party organizations, documents the Soviet Union's assistance to flood victims in the Po valley—the setting of Rossellini's episode about the partisan resistance in *Paisà*. Other early subjects for Pontecorvo include a Roman market in *Porta portese/Portese Gate* (1954); a Roman dog kennel in *Cani dietro le sbarre/Dogs behind Bars* (1954); a popular festival in *Festa a Castelluccio/Festival at Castelluccio* (1955); marble cutters in *Uomini di marmo/Men of Marble* (1955); and the decline of a community that depended on a closed sulfur mine in *Pane e zolfo/Bread and Sulfur* (1956).

Pontecorvo's early documentaries in the neorealist style were actually a throwback to the earliest postwar period of neorealism. Pontecorvo made documentary films that depicted the reality of postwar Italy after his experience as an actor in Vergano's *Outcry* as Pietro the resistance fighter, a role that was true to his own life experiences. However, when Pontecorvo began to make his short, government-subsidized films in the neorealist style in the early 1950s, the founders of the Italian neorealist school or style had moved away from the style and format of Italian naturalism, or *verismo*, toward experimentation in art film or in more commercial cinema. For example, instead of continuing in the vein of socially relevant drama about fishermen, such as *La terra trema/The Earth Trembles* (1948), in 1954 Luchino Visconti made *Senso/The Wanton Countess* (1954), a love story involving an Austrian deserter and a Venetian countess set during the wars for Italian unification in the 1860s. Rossellini moved away from the wartime themes of his pre- and postwar films, such as *L'uomo dalla croce/Man of the Cross* (1943) and *Rome Open City* (1945), to films focused on spiritual quests starring Ingrid Bergman, such as *Europa '51* (1952), *Viaggio in Italia/Voyage to Italy* (1953), and *Giovanna d'Arco al rogo/Joan of Arc* (1954). Even an ideologically committed director like Giuseppe De Santis, who had appeared with Pontecorvo in Vergano's *Outcry* and who remained in the Italian Communist Party (PCI) even after successive Soviet repressions of independence movements in Eastern Europe, made a melodrama about a fallen woman, *Un marito per Anna Zaccheo/A Husband for Anna Zaccheo* (1953), and *Giorni d'amore/Days of Love* (1954), a sentimental tale starring Marcello Mastroianni. These efforts are far from the sort of melodrama within larger historical events that De Santis made during the immediate aftermath of the war, such as *Caccia tragica/Bitter Hunt* (1946). Arguably the last neorealist film, De Sica's *Il tetto/The Roof* (1956), came years after public and box office results had begun to reward more commercial forms of entertainment with concessions to popular taste. De Sica had also moved from his neorealist moment of *The Bicycle Thief* to more commercial films, such as *L'oro di Napoli/The Gold of Naples* (1954), starring the latest revelation of the Miss Italy beauty pageant, Sophia Loren, and comedian Totò (Antonio De Curtis). Despite the period of neorealism after the war, the popular trends in Italian film did not change greatly from the 1930s to the 1950s, with a steady flow of peplum epics, melodramas, historical dramas, and romantic comedies.[20]

Pontecorvo's entrance into cinema coincided with the debates over Italian neorealism in the mid-1950s, which had an impact on Pontecorvo's future work as a filmmaker. By the early 1950s the resistance coalition of Catholics, communists, monarchists, and republicans had broken down in the Cold War bipolarism that dominated international politics. As wartime themes began to wane, many neorealist films were perceived as box office disappointments in Italy, even though Rossellini's *Rome Open City* was the top Italian domestic film in 1945, Rossellini's *Paisà* was seventh and Vergano's *Outcry* was the ninth in 1946, and De Sica's *The Bicycle Thief* was fifth in 1948.[21] The critical appeal of neorealist films was actually heightened in Italy due to success abroad. De Sica's *Sciuscià/Shoeshine* (1946) and *The Bicycle Thief* and Rossellini's *Rome Open City* all won prestigious foreign film awards in the United States and in France.[22]

As neorealism declined, a barrage of leftist criticism, following a tradition in Italian intellectualism of setting social and cultural agendas, attempted to keep the focus of an already expiring neorealism on class issues. Left-wing critics such as Guido Aristarco saw an abandonment of the early heroic neorealism of the immediate postwar period due to the diminishing political activism of the historic group of neorealist filmmakers (Rossellini, De Sica, Visconti). In fact films from 1950 to 1951—like Rossellini's *Francesco Giullare di Dio/The Flowers of St. Francis* (1950), Visconti's *Bellissima*, Fellini's *Luci del varietà/Variety Lights* (1950), or De Sica's *Miracolo a Milano/Miracle in Milan* (1951)—seem less politically motivated than earlier neorealist films. With the box office disappointment of De Sica's *Umberto D.* (1952), the fortunes of neorealism declined irrevocably. There was governmental hostility from Christian Democrat–led coalitions; this hostility is best indicated by then minister Giulio Andreotti's famous remark about not wishing to see Italy's dirty linen washed in public in reaction to De Sica's *Umberto D.* Such governmental reaction was important, as Italian films—including the shorts Pontecorvo would make in the early 1950s—were allotted tax breaks and subsidies for artistic merit that were bestowed at the discretion of government officials like Andreotti.[23]

Yet the decline of the fortunes of the neorealist school came during a political awakening for Gillo. Pontecorvo's brother Bruno Pontecorvo, the physicist, defected to work on the Soviet nuclear arms program in 1950.[24] Bruno later admitted his actions were the result of a sort of religious crisis caused by his extremely rational existence as a physicist. To his later regret, Bruno Pontecorvo was eventually so absorbed by Soviet propaganda that he has stated that he was able to rationalize such horrific crimes as the forced starvation of the Kulaks and Ukrainian farmers in the forced collectivization of farms in the 1930s.[25] With a brother working to develop the Soviet hydrogen bomb and his own credentials as a wartime resistance leader in the communist brigades, Gillo seemed to be set in his ideological convictions. However, true to the rebellious nature he had displayed as a child, Gillo was not so easily controlled. Despite his connections among the elite of the Italian Communist Party and his brother's defection to work on the Soviet nuclear arms program, Gillo took a more independent approach to politics and left the PCI in 1956 following the Soviet invasion of Hungary. Pontecorvo's move was not uncommon among Italian leftists at the time. The repression of the Hungarian revolution by Soviet troops had political repercussions in Italy; it caused a further split between Palmiro Togliatti's pro-Moscow PCI and Pietro Nenni's more independent-minded Italian Socialist Party (PSI). By leaving the PCI Pontecorvo followed his conscience, as he felt unable to remain associated with a party structure whose monolithic authority he had perhaps naively accepted as a result of his heady days with his brother's comrades in prewar Paris and his subsequent experiences in the anti-Nazi/ Fascist resistance in Italy. Pontecorvo had believed, again perhaps naively, and despite the maturity he had reached in age (in 1956 Pontecorvo was already thirty-seven), in party rhetoric about the creation of a new man and new sense of political and moral consciousness in a classless society. The rhetoric of collective identity versus individualism derived from Marxist ideology would still dominate Pontecorvo's films. But when Russian troops repressed the Hungarian independence movement in 1956, Pontecorvo had the intellectual clarity and above all the courage to question, and eventually reject, the hierarchical structure of the PCI and its insistence on the paradoxical idea of what he has defined as "democratic centralism."[26] Pontecorvo was able to reject the simplistic myths of the working class as the arbiter of intellectual or artistic controversy and the Soviet Union as a model society. He demonstrated a keen eye for discerning political reality, although idealistic adhesion to left-wing revolutionary politics would remain an important element in his films and personal political convictions.

At around the time of his entry into documentary filmmaking, Pontecorvo met his future screenwriting partner, Franco Solinas (1927–1982), whose political outlook was similar to Pontecorvo's own. Solinas began working with Pontecorvo on *Giovanna* (1955) and would coauthor all of Pontecorvo's features— despite the partners' often colorful rows—until *Ogro* (1979), the only feature Pontecorvo would make without Solinas. Many of Solinas's screenplays were referred to Pontecorvo, including his adaptation of the Pier Paolo Pasolini novella *Ragazzi di Vita: Una Vita violenta/A Violent Life* (1962); *¿Quien sabe?/A Bullet for the General* (1967), by Damiano Damiani; *Il Mercenario/The Mercenary* (1968), eventually directed by Sergio Corbucci; and *Monsieur Klein/Mr. Klein* (1976), by Joseph Losey. Besides collaborating with Pontecorvo, Solinas worked with other important filmmakers, including with Rossellini on an adaptation of a Stendhal story, *Vanina Vanini/The Betrayer* (1961), with Francesco

Rosi on a biopic of the mysterious Sicilian bandit *Salvatore Giuliano* (1962), with Costa Gavras on his political films *Etat de siège/State of Siege* (1973) and *Hanna K.* (1983), and with Joseph Losey on *The Assassination of Trotsky* (1972) and *Monsieur Klein/Mr. Klein* (1976), a film that Pontecorvo had actually co-scripted with Solinas and then declined to direct.[27] In the late 1960s Solinas would pen a number of political westerns, an offshoot of the spaghetti western genre, which attracted producer interest after the box office success of Sergio Leone's films starring Clint Eastwood—*Un pugno di dollars/A Fistful of Dollars* (1964), *Per qualche dollaro in più/For a Few Dollars More* (1965), *Il buono, il brutto, e il cattivo/The Good, the Bad, and the Ugly* (1966).

It was during this year (1956) of political awakening that Pontecorvo began his filmmaking career in earnest. He was invited to contribute to Dutch filmmaker Joris Iven's *Die Windrose/Rose of the Winds* (1956), a collection of shorts on women's issues commissioned by the Women's International Democratic Federation and the Woman's International Democratic Federation of then East Germany. Pontecorvo's political connections to the Italian and international Left, and his ability to complete documentaries that received government artistic merit subsidies, made him a perfect candidate to direct an episode in Iven's film. Pontecorvo's contribution, *Giovanna*, is about a group of Italian women who strike at a textile mill. The film treated themes of feminist liberation well before such issues were commonplace and gave Pontecorvo an opportunity to use his experiences making documentary films in a longer format.

With *Giovanna*, Pontecorvo officially entered into the ranks of professional film directors. He subsequently received an offer to direct a feature, *La grande strada azzurra/The Wide Blue Road* (1957) based on Solinas's novel about Sardinian fishermen entitled *Squarciò* (*Squarciò the Fisherman*). Solinas's story recalls the plot of Sicilian author Giovanni Verga's *I Malavoglia/The House by the Meddlar Tree*, the source for Luchino Visconti's canonical neorealist film *La terra trema/The Earth Trembles* (1948). *The Wide Blue Road* presents the struggles of a fishing community in Sardinia attempting to form a cooperative against middlemen who exploit the fishermen's labor by driving down the price of their daily catch. With the opportunity to direct a feature came the threat of compromise to Pontecorvo's purist approach to filmmaking. True to his grounding in the neorealist style, Pontecorvo initially balked when producers indicated their plans for the film to be shot in color and feature the well-known actors Yves Montand and Alida Valli. The resulting film, *The Wide Blue Road*, is an example of what later became known as "pink neorealism." In pink neorealism the basic elements of the neorealist style—such as a simple plot with a progressive theme—are maintained, with nods to audience demands for more visually pleasing elements such as recognizable stars and color. Despite the compromises, Pontecorvo was rewarded when the film won the best director award at the Karlovy Vary festival in Russia, although it must be mentioned that he won the prize during a period when his brother Bruno was a star in the Soviet nuclear arms program.

Two years later, again collaborating with Solinas, Pontecorvo took up the theme of survival in a Nazi concentration camp in *Kapò* (1959). The film is the story of a Jewish girl from Paris, deported to a Nazi death camp, who assumes the identity of a political prisoner and then collaborates with the Nazis as a camp trustee or kapò. For the film Pontecorvo sought inspiration in *Se questo è un uomo/Survival in Auschwitz*, an account of the Holocaust by Italian author and Auschwitz survivor Primo Levi. In working on *Kapò* Pontecorvo and Solinas continued to struggle with the legacy of neorealist style, as well as with to the producer's decision to cast American actress Susan Strasberg, daughter of the then head of the New York Actors Studio, Lee Stasberg, in the starring role. The Academy Award–nominated film caused controversy regarding the recursion to an unlikely love story between the kapò played by Strasburg and a Russian prisoner of war, played by Laurent Terzieff.

After *Kapò*, Pontecorvo would not release another film for six years. Pontecorvo has explained the pattern of long delays between projects as a result of his inability to accept any form of compromise or middle ground in his commitment to a project, although this purported reticence may actually have been a function of his age. Like Michelangelo Antonioni—who made his first feature, *Story of a Love Affair* (1950), at age thirty-eight—Pontecorvo became a director after a brief stint as a journalist. Pontecorvo also debuted with *The Wide Blue Road* at age thirty-eight and made *Kapò* when he was forty. Thus Pontecorvo came to the cinema in full middle age after having lived through enough experiences for a lifetime: as tennis pro, as resistance fighter in World War II, and as a journalist in the early postwar period. Like other future directors who appeared in Aldo Vergano's *Outcry* (Francesco De Santis and Carlo Lizzani), Pontecorvo was a late arrival on the neorealist scene; he was ten to twenty years younger than the generation of directors—among them Rossellini, De Sica, and Visconti—who were the pioneers of the Italian neorealist style. Pontecorvo was too young to have learned his craft in the Italian studio system of the 1930s, like Roberto Rossellini or Vittorio De Sica. This chronological separation from the main period of neorealism did not hinder other directors: Francesco Rosi (born in 1922), like Pontecorvo, became an important political film director; Federico Fellini (born in 1920) used his experiences working as an assistant director and screenwriter for Rossellini to become an important art cinema director; Sergio Leone (born in 1921) went from assistant director on Vittorio De Sica's *The Bicycle Thief* to become the master of the Italian western. Throughout his career Pontecorvo seems to have had difficulty adapting to the rhythms of commercial cinema. Pontecorvo began his career by accepting compromises to his ideal of the cinema, such as the stars and color film in *The Wide Blue Road*. He then agreed to include a love story between a Nazi kapò and a Russian prisoner of war in *Kapò* on the insistence of his writing partner, Franco Solinas.[28] But after receiving international recognition for *Kapò* (including an Oscar nomination), Pontecorvo would be increasingly wary of compromise, and he would withdraw from many worthy film projects. Other important directors also completed few films, although it is a condition more excusable in places with lower film output, like the countries of Scandinavia in the careers of noted masters like Denmark's Carl Dreyer or Finland's Nyrki Tapiovaara. Pontecorvo had come to maturity as an internationally recognized and Academy Award–nominated director with *Kapò* by 1960, a year when the Italian film industry was second only to Hollywood in terms of the number of films produced. Unlike his writing partner, Solinas, who penned a number of politically themed westerns and political films, Pontecorvo was unable or perhaps unwilling to find a continuous niche within the Italian film industry during its years of greatest production opportunity. Pontecorvo's low output is one of the great missed opportunities of Italian film history. During his later years, it has been speculated, Pontecorvo actually earned his living by shooting television commercials and accepting bureaucratic postings in Italian cultural institutions, such as director of the Venice film festival and president of the state-run Cinecittà cinema studios in Rome.[29]

Pontecorvo has explained his attitude in terms of a lack of ambition and inability to complete a project that did not capture his unequivocal interest. However, other statements point to an adhesion to an idea of artistic creation as a pure process whose roots are outside left-wing political ideology, or to the theoretical ramifications of works by authors that Pontecorvo has cited as influences, such as Umberto Barbaro, Georg Lukacs, or Antonio Gramsci. In a late interview Pontecorvo admitted to an unexpected sense of solidarity with the aesthetic ideas of Italian idealist and liberal philosopher Benedetto Croce (1866–1952), who held that art is a cosmic experience that relies on intuitive sensibility.

Pontecorvo has stated that he does not consider himself a Crocean, yet he is completely convinced by the definition in Crocean aesthetics in which artistic intuition is an *a priori* synthesis of form and content. According to Pontecorvo, film fits into this concept of art, particularly film with an artistic mission that may be born from an intuition that has the essence of a story or plot that leads to the development of the style and the way in which it may be recounted. According to Pontecorvo, this intuition extends also to the manner in which a film may be photographed and even accompanied by music. Pontecorvo has stated that he feels the task of a director is to follow this intuition without abandoning it and resisting all influences, pressures, and problems that come up in the profession. Pontecorvo would extend this idea of the primacy of intuition to an insistence that a director should not allow himself or herself to be swayed by ideas that appear in the script writing phase if they might deviate from the original intuition.[30]

When asked about his cinematic origins, Pontecorvo has claimed that he owes more to Rossellini and to the montage-influenced style of certain Soviet directors, such as Sergei Eisenstein and Nicolai Eck, than to neorealism, arriving at the equation that his model is three-quarters Rossellini and one-fourth Eisenstein, Vsevolod Pudovkin, and in particular the seminal Ukrainian director Aleksandr Dovzhenko, whose early silent films *Zvenigora* (1928), *Arsenal* (1928), and *Earth* (1930) have elements of the collective versus individual narrative mixed with nationalism (in this case Ukrainian national identity), which are central to the plots of Pontecorvo's early feature films.[31] Certainly Pontecorvo's fondness for montages of anonymous faces in crowds to represent his interpretation of the pulse of the populace during key moments of films like *The Battle of Algiers* point to an influence from Soviet formalist directors. From his appearance in Vergano's *Outcry* Pontecorvo has a direct line to the Italian professional cinema of the 1930s and directors like Alessandro Blasetti and Mario Camerini, who were also influenced by the film style of Soviet formalism and montage.[32] A Crocean search for artistic purity also exists in the work of important neorealist directors. Rossellini's working methods and disdain for technical planning hint of a Crocean search for the cosmic, as does his improvisation of narrative. The prevalence of mystical experience in Rossellini's films and even his preference for long shots over montage reflect a clear philosophical attitude that approaches a Crocean mistrust of technical wizardry. Even in the epic, early Rossellini of the war trilogy (*Rome Open City, Paisà, Germany Year Zero*), screenwriter Cesare Amidei's leftist orthodoxy was countered by the comedy and spiritualism of the other screenwriter, Federico Fellini.[33] The elements that Pontecorvo counts as vital in his origins as a director—the use of naturalistic elements in filmmaking such as nonprofessional actors and on-location shooting, and an interest in Soviet montage-based symbolism in order to portray emotional and even political elements—were already an inherent part of the Italian professional cinematic style in the 1930s. But Pontecorvo's stubborn insistence on the purity of his artistic process also belies a latent Crocean sensibility, as Pontecorvo himself has stated in the interview cited above.

In 1963 in Rome, after completing *Kapò*, Pontecorvo collaborated with his assistant director from *Cani dietro le sbarre/Dogs behind Bars* (1954), Fausta Leoni, on a proposal for a series of television programs on the paranormal, magic, and near-death experiences. The script was later published as an appendix to Leoni's 1969 book on the paranormal, *Karma storia autentica di una reincarnazione/Karma: The Story of an Authentic Reincarnation*. Pontecorvo and Leoni proposed the series for RAI, the Italian state television network, which promptly rejected it. Yet the remaining treatment gives a precise indication of ideological and personal points important to Pontecorvo and his attraction to themes beyond the materialistic and deterministic scope of left-wing ideology. The script for *Karma* alternates between various man-on-the-street interviews in which the camera crew approaches people to ask questions (out of the blue) on the meaning of life. The interviewer receives responses that run from mild hostility to attempts to deflect questions that have no complete answer. The first episode was to include a montage of images that relate to the theme of the mystery of death and the afterlife, with subjects including a funeral in the deep Italian south, interviews in an Italian prison, scenes from popular festivals like the Day of the Dead in Mexico, and scenes from films like Eisenstein's *Que viva Mexico* (1932) and Jean Epstein's *The Fall of the House of Usher* (1928). The documentary was to have a sound track demonstrating Pontecorvo's interest in music, with excerpts from Stravinsky's *Appollon Musagete* and Brahms's *Requiem*. The next episodes were to introduce excerpts from works by famed writers like Tolstoy, Dickinson, Natalia Ginzburg, and Aldous Huxley about the eternal questions of human existence.

After *Kapò* was nominated for an Oscar, Pontecorvo reportedly received offers from around the world. Instead, for his next project Pontecorvo chose a subject that would be his masterwork. *The Battle of Algiers* (1966), banned by the French government until 1971, depicts the Algerian struggle for independence from France and has become one of the most influential films in cinema history, used not only by aspiring filmmakers but even by terrorist and antiterrorist organizations as a training film. The film re-creates the cinematic style of the heroic neorealist period with thematic input that recalls Pontecorvo's memories of clandestine, armed struggle from his past as a resistance fighter. There are also contributions from Yacef Saadi, a leader of the Algerian resistance in the city of Algiers, who plays himself and received a writing credit in the film. *The Battle of Algiers* was a critical and commercial success, with awards from the Venice Film Festival and another nomination for two Academy Awards including best director.

The attention that Pontecorvo received from *The Battle of Algiers* again raised the interest of Hollywood producers who, with Italian producer Alberto Grimaldi, were eager to have him direct an action adventure film, or even a western. With *Burn!* (1969), Pontecorvo was able to command a big budget production with an international star, Marlon Brando, in a film that continues his investigation of third world issues. Unfortunately *Burn!* was poorly received outside of Italy and critically, which led to another period of prolonged artistic inactivity for Pontecorvo. He would not direct again until *Ogro* (1979), Pontecorvo's last feature film, which depicts the assassination of the Francoist prime minister, Carrero Blanco, by ETA Basque separatists in 1973. The film was made in 1978, a year in which Italy was traumatized by the kidnapping and murder of the former prime minister Aldo Moro by Italian communist terrorists, the Red Brigades. Due to events in Italy, Pontecorvo reconsidered his stance on political violence and changed the ending of *Ogro* in order to question the legitimacy of violent armed struggle.

Despite receiving offers to direct and planning a number of projects himself, over the last quarter century of his life Pontecorvo steadfastly refused to return to the director's chair as a feature film director. After *Ogro*, Pontecorvo was unable to apply the themes of armed struggle and resistance with the sort of ideological approach that had characterized his previous features. Pontecorvo's last, great, unfinished project, *Il tempo della fine/The Time of the End*, was to be a film about Jesus portrayed as a lay, revolutionary figure, who eventually disappoints the residents of Jerusalem, since his message is spiritual and ethical rather than military.[34]

The projects that Pontecorvo did manage to complete were documentaries and shorts that demonstrate a spirit of resignation and ideological uncertainty. In the documentary *Ritorno ad Algeri/Return to Algiers* (1992), an aging Pontecorvo, at seventy-three, returns to Algiers to as a journalist to witness that country's struggle with Islamic fundamentalism and civil war. In the short *Nostalgia di protezione: Danza della fata confetto/Protection Nostalgia: Dance of the Sugar Plum Fairy* (1997), a Roman businessman yearns for the security he experienced as a child protected by his mother. These last efforts from Pontecorvo are witness to the insecurity and self-doubt about the themes of armed struggle and revolution that surfaced when he was forced to change the tone of *Ogro* during the period of the Moro murder in 1978. Pontecorvo's inability to complete a feature film after *Ogro* and the subject matter of the documentaries and shorts that he did complete reveal the moral dilemma inherent in trying to classify diverse violent struggles as terrorism or freedom fighting, a determination dependent on political and cultural preconceptions. After *Ogro*, Pontecorvo moved from the ideological certainty about armed struggle and self-sacrifice that had been defining features of films like *Outcry* and *The Battle of Algiers*.

Besides making two important short films—*Return to Algiers* (1992) and *Protection Nostalgia* (1997)—Pontecorvo's activity as a filmmaker in the last period of his life was largely limited to the making of television commercials or short documentaries for Italian industries like the Italian national energy consortium, ENI. One of Pontecorvo's last film efforts was actually a tourist film about the wonders of Italy, *12 registi per 12 città/12 Directors for 12 Cities* (1998), in which the aging director presents a postcard of the northeastern

Italian city of Udine. Pontecorvo also promoted a quixotic effort to create a cultural unity between the film industries of Latin countries in order to counter the distribution power of Hollywood. Pontecorvo had also been slated to participate in a collaborative documentary: directors including Antonioni, Bernardo Bertolucci, and Pontecorvo's fellow actor from *Outcry* Carlo Lizzani, placed their crews in Italian cities in anticipation of riots by the antiglobal movement's demonstrations against the 2001 G8 conference in Genoa. But Pontecorvo was forced to withdraw due to back pain.[35]

NOTES

1. Irene Bignardi, *Memorie estorte a uno smemorato vita di Gillo Pontecorvo* (Milan: Feltrinelli, 1999), 1–34.

2. Gillo Pontecorvo, "Interview," *Kapò*, DVD (Rome: Cristaldi Film, 2003).

3. See Miriam Mafai, *Il lungo freddo: Storia di Bruno Pontecorvo lo scienzato che scelse l'URSS* (Milan: A. Mondadori, 1992).

4. Bignardi, *Memorie*, 1–34.

5. Luigi Cipriani, M. Conciatori, M. Giraldi, and L. Ricci, eds., *Primo piano sull'autore Gillo Pontecorvo "La dittatura della verità"* (Rome: Designer, 1999), 15–34.

6. Bignardi, *Memorie*, 40–58.

7. Bignardi, *Memorie*, 13.

8. See Enzo Collotti, *Il fascismo e gli ebrei: Le leggi razziali in Italia* (Rome: Laterza, 2003).

9. Bignardi, *Memorie*, 106.

10. OVRA is the Italian acronym for *Organizzazione per la Vigilanza e la Repressione dell'Antifascismo*—Organization for the Oversight and Repression of Anti-Fascism. Bignardi, *Memorie*, 40–58.

11. Bignardi, *Memorie*, 50–58.

12. Carlo Celli, "Interview with Marcello Pezzetti," *Critical Inquiry*, Autumn 27, 2000, 155.

13. Bignardi, *Memorie*, 69.

14. Carlo Celli, "Aldo Vergano's *Il sole sorge ancora/Outcry* (1946) as Influence on Gillo Pontecorvo," *Forum Italicum* 38, no. 1 (Spring 2004): 217–28.

15. Bignardi, *Memorie*, 59–81.

16. Massimo Ghirelli, *Gillo Pontecorvo (Il castoro cinema)* (Firenze, Italy: La Nuova Italia, 1978), 3.

17. Paolo D'Agostini, "La lunga strada della libertà," in Cipriani, Conciatori, Giraldi, and Ricci, *Primo piano*, 37–46.

18. Alessandro Levantesi, "Intervista," in Cipriani, Conciatori, Giraldi, and Ricci, *Primo piano*, 22.

19. Massimo Ghirelli, *Gillo Pontecorvo (Il castoro cinema)* (Firenze, Italy: La Nuova Italia, 1978), 3.

20. Pam Cook, *The Cinema Book: A Complete Guide to Understanding the Movies*, 1st ed. (New York: Pantheon, 1985), 39.

21. Maurizio Baroni, *Platea in piedi, 1945–1958: Manifesti e dati statistici del cinema italiano; testi a cura di Valerio M. Manfredi* (Bologna, Italy: Bolelli Editore, 1995–1999).

22. Gianfranco Casadio, *Adultere, Fedifraghe, Innocenti: La donna del "neorealismo popolare" nel cinema italiano degli anni Cinquanta* (Ravenna, Italy: Longo Editore, 1990).

23. See Casadio, *Adultere*.

24. See Miriam Mafai, *Il lungo freddo: Storia di Bruno Pontecorvo, lo scienziato che scelse l'URSS* (Milan: A. Mondadori, 1992).

25. Bignardi, *Memorie*, 74.

26. Bignardi, *Memorie*, 89.

27. Cipriani, Conciatori, Giraldi, and Ricci, *Primo piano*, 29.

28. Pontecorvo, "Interview," *Kapò*, DVD.

29. Edward Said, "The Quest for Gillo Pontecorvo," *Interview* 18, no. 11 (November 1988): 90–93.

30. Bignardi, *Memorie*, 159 (translation mine).

31. Franco Solinas, *Gillo Pontecorvo's "The Battle of Algiers": A Film Written by Franco Solinas*, ed. Pier Nico (New York: Scribner, 1973), 173.

32. Francesco Savio, "Mario Camerini," in *Cinecittà anni trenta: Parlano 116 protagonisti del secondo cinema italiano (1930–1943)*, ed. Tulio Kezich (Rome: Bulzoni, 1979), 225.

33. Carlo Celli, "Critical and Philosophical Discussions regarding Italian Neo-Realism," *Romance Languages Annual* 7 (1995): 222–26.

34. Franco Bolzoni, "Un film su Gesù conversazione di Gillo Pontecorvo con Francesco Bulzoni," in Cipriani, Conciatori, Giraldi, and Ricci, *Primo piano*, 133–39.

35. Patrick Kennedy, "One Deadly Summit," *Sight and Sound*, 2001, 28–29.

• 1 •

Pontecorvo and Aldo Vergano's
Il sole sorge ancora/Outcry (1946)[1]

$\mathscr{P}$ontecorvo has claimed that the film that directly inspired him to become a director was Rossellini's *Paisà/Paisan* (1946). Rossellini's film obviously evoked memories of Pontecorvo's heroic experiences in the Italian resistance.[2] Rossellini's film has also been cited as a great influence on the French new wave of the late 1950s and early 1960s—directors like Francois Truffaut were inspired by French critic Andre Bazin's praise of the film and of the style of Italian neorealism in general. However, another film, Aldo Vergano's *Il sole sorge ancora/Outcry* (1946), seems to have had a greater impact on Pontecorvo's cinematic formation, as it contains specific approaches to acting, settings, lighting, cinematic style, plot lines, and characterization that recur throughout Pontecorvo's films.

Although well known in Italy as one of the standard bearers of the neorealist style, Vergano's 1946 film never enjoyed wide public or critical recognition abroad, particularly in comparison to more renowned neorealist films of the same period. Perhaps because of its uncompromisingly rhetorical tone, the film is largely unknown outside Italy despite serving as a training ground for many influential Italian filmmakers of the postwar period, including Pontecorvo, Carlo Lizzani, and Giuseppe De Santis. Vergano adapted themes from his experiences in the Italian professional cinema of the 1930s and early 1940s in *Outcry* that had an important if unrecognized influence on the work of Pontecorvo.

Based in Milan and funded in part by a partisan veterans' association, the Associazione Nationale Partigiana Italiana (ANPI), *Outcry* depicts the moral, social, and political impetus for the partisan movement and features direct input from active participants in the resistance, including Pontecorvo.[3] The producers' first choice for director was Goffredo Alessandrini, later discarded because of his

1

reputation as a Fascist-era filmmaker.[4] Alessandrini's last film before the war, *Abuna Messias/Cardinal Messias* (1939) won the Mussolini Cup for best Italian film at the Venice Film Festival in 1940. Vergano was chosen to direct *Outcry* because his political inclinations would better reflect those of the ANPI. Despite his progressive politics, Vergano had been able to find work in the prewar Italian film industry, as his family and educational background proved valuable in his dealings with the regime. Important figures in the regime, such as culture czar Luigi Freddi and Mussolini's doomed son-in-law Galeazzo Ciano, were reportedly aware of Vergano's political leanings and yet tolerated his presence in the Italian film industry for apparently personal reasons.[5]

Vergano's first important credit as screenwriter was on Alessandro Blasetti's *Sole* (1929), a lost classic of the Italian silent period, which depicts fishermen, shepherds, and peasants working courageously on the regime's irrigation and land reclamation projects in the Pontine region south of Rome.[6] *Sole* was hailed as a rebirth for Italian cinema, especially for its use of nonprofessional actors and popular themes, a characteristic of the *verismo* (naturalism) current in Italian literature that would be echoed in Italian neorealism in the 1940s. Vergano also aided Blasetti on the seminal journal *Cinema*, founded by Mussolini's son Vittorio, which became a stopping ground for many future directors, including Michelangelo Antonioni and Luchino Visconti. In his critical writings Blasetti praised the style and work of Russian directors such as Eisenstein and Pudovkin and saw their thematic emphasis on heroic collectivity as a model for the revitalization of the Italian film industry.[7] Blasetti's directorial efforts, like *1860/Gesuzza the Garibaldian Wife* (1933) borrow from Russian cinema, with a photographic style and story lines that emphasize the relationship between characters and their natural surroundings.

Vergano actually worked as a screenwriter on several films by Goffredo Alessandrini, the director he would supplant on *Outcry*. Alessandrini was best known for his Fascist-era war films featuring matinee idol Amadeo Nazzari. Vergano was the unit manager on Nazzari's debut *Ginevra degli Almieri* (1936) and the screenwriter on *Cavalleria* (1936), a Nazzari vehicle that combines a love story and social tensions amidst World War I heroics. Vergano also collaborated on the screenplay of *Don Bosco* (1935) with Alessandrini and Sergio Amidei, later known for his work on Rossellini's *Roma città aperta/Rome Open City* (1945).[8] Vergano worked with Amidei again on *La notte delle beffe/The Night of Tricks* (1940), another Nazzari vehicle, which ran into some difficulty with regime censors for its portrayal of social issues. Other Vergano credits include Mario Bonnard's *L'Albero di Adamo/Adam's Tree* (1936), a romantic comedy that includes a writing credit for Corrado Alvaro, an author best known for his novels in the naturalistic *verismo* tradition.

Vergano was also coscreenwriter with Cesare Zavattini, best known for his neorealist collaborations with Vittorio De Sica, on *San Giovanni decollato/St. John the Baptist Beheaded* (1940), a vehicle for Italian comedian Totò (Antonio De Curtis) with themes of class tension, directed by Amleto Palmieri.

Vergano debuted as director with another screenplay collaboration with Amidei, *Pietro Micca* (1939), a remake of a historical drama about the Piedmontese defense against a Franco-Hispanic invasion in 1706 in which the humble miner Pietro Micca blows himself up in order to deliver the city. This theme of self-sacrifice and suicide for political reasons would resonate in *Outcry* as well as in the films of Giuseppe De Santis, such as *Caccia tragica/Bitter Hunt* (1946), and in the political films of Pontecorvo, like *Kapò* (1960), *La battaglia di Algeri/The Battle of Algiers* (1966), and *Queimada!/Burn!* (1969). Vergano's other prewar directing credits include *I figli della notte/Los hijos de la noche* (1939), with Spanish director Benito Perojo; and *Quelli della montagna* (1943), another Amadeo Nazzari vehicle. Vergano worked with Blasetti on a screenplay for *Quelli della montagna*, which mixes elements of sentimental drama with the propaganda film by glorifying the exploits of the Italian alpine mountain troops. The conclusion to be drawn from Vergano's prewar filmography is that by the time he directed *Outcry* in the winter of 1945–1946, he was a seasoned professional in the Italian cinema like his colleagues Rossellini and De Sica, who later gained international fame as neorealist icons.[9]

The style and even the subject matter of Vergano's early films carry over into *Outcry*. The story line recalls the emphasis on collective efforts and love triangles in Blasetti's *Sole*, the political suicide in *Pietro Micca*, the forced heroism in Amadeo Nazzari vehicles. Besides the influence on Vergano of Blasetti, *Outcry* benefited from Aldo Tonti's cinematography. Tonti, like Vergano, had worked in the prewar Italian professional cinema, on films such as Alessandrini's *Abuna Messias*, Visconti's *Ossessione/Obsession* (1943), and De Sica's wartime film *La porta del cielo/The Gate of Heaven* (1966). In each of these films Tonti overcame conditions that would presage the methods and stylistic necessities of neorealism. For example, *Abuna Messias* was shot on location in the Cobbù plain and Cercer mountain chain in Ethiopia.[10] *Ossessione* is often cited as the first neorealist film not only because of the subject matter but also because of the unadorned quality of its photography. Filming on De Sica's *The Gate of Heaven* took place under precarious conditions in Nazi-occupied Rome.[11] Under Tonti's influence Vergano's film *Outcry* has a rough newsreel quality that would become a neorealist commonplace and was adopted as a cinematic style by Pontecorvo. Pontecorvo's early documentaries—*La Missione Timiriazev/The Timiriazev Mission* (1953), about a flood on the Po River; *Cani dietro le sbarre/Dogs behind Bars* (1954), about dog kennels in Rome; *Pane e zolfo/Bread and Sulfur* (1956)

about the closing of sulfur mines—were made in the style and under the influence of neorealism, which favored a stark, unadorned cinematography. This style
would carry over into Pontecorvo's features, including *Giovanna* (1956) and especially *The Battle of Algiers* (1966), which actually had to be advertised as a film
that did not use newsreel footage. Audiences mistakenly assumed it was a documentary film because of Pontecorvo's impeccable mimicry of a documentary
style.

For the female lead in *Outcry* producers reportedly contacted Clara
Calamai, who had appeared for Vergano on *Pietro Micca* and for Visconti on
Ossessione. However, she reportedly declined in order to appear in Mario
Camerini's undervalued *Due letter anonime/Two Anonymous Letters* (1945).
Nevertheless, the cast did have experience in the cinema. Elli Parvo (Matilde)
had been the female lead in Rossellini and Marcello Pagilero's
Desiderio/Women (1946). Vittorio Duse (Cesare) had a brief role in Visconti's
Ossessione. Carlo Lizzani (Don Camillo) would become a director whose
credits would include the Italian Holocaust drama *L'oro di Roma/The Gold of
Rome* (1961) and *Mussolini ultimo atto/The Last Days of Mussolini* (1974).
Tonino, the count's servant, is played by Giuseppe De Santis, another future
director whose credits would include *Caccia tragica/Bitter Hunt* (1946) and
Riso amaro/Bitter Rice (1949). Pontecorvo plays Pietro, a courageous and
doomed partisan. Vergano himself plays a railway worker. The rest of the cast
was taken from acquaintances and nonprofessional actors, in the neorealist
style. Filming began in the winter of 1945–1946 on location in the Po valley,
where the memory of the resistance was extremely fresh.[12]

The film opens with a sequence set in a bordello filled with Italian soldiers on leave; they are surprised by the radio announcement of the Italian
monarchy's decision (taken on September 8, 1943) to switch to the Allied side
in the war. A German dragnet for Italian soldiers who have abandoned their
army units follows. The protagonist, Cesare, is an Italian soldier who has just
enjoyed the services of Mariska, a prostitute who invites him to remain despite the commotion of his panicking comrades. With this scene the film
clearly annunciates the opinion that on September 8 the Italian army was
caught with its pants down. This refers not just to the mismanagement of the
war by the regime, but also to the confusion that followed the Italian king's
decision to switch to the Allied side, arrest Mussolini, set up a government in
Brindisi, and assign World War I hero general Badoglio with the task of join-
ing royalist troops with the other anti-Fascist political and military factions of
the Commitato per la Liberazione Nazionale (Committee for National Liberation, CLN).

In this opening bordello scene, the film makes an initial equation between illicit sex and defeat, an impression reinforced further when Cesare

abandons his army unit and returns home to the Po valley as a civilian. At home, Cesare encounters two possible love interests who offer opposing models of womanhood. His childhood sweetheart, Laura, a name that recalls the literary topos of the angelic woman, is identified with moral rectitude. Throughout the film she is depicted carrying children at the hearth as a traditional female representing the home and family values. In contrast, Matilde is the emancipated wife of the local factory owner. She drinks, smokes, listens to jazz, has a semilesbian relationship with her cousin, and keeps a male personal trainer, Spartaco, who poses for her to paint his abstract portrait. The Matilde character is very much in the tradition of the *telefono bianco* (white telephone) romantic comedies developed in the 1930s and 1940s—films such as Bonnard's *Io suo padre* (1938), in which a young boxer is tempted by a *fatalona* (femme fatale) played by Clara Calamai.[13] Vergano would have been practiced in the commonplaces surrounding the *fatalona* stock character, as he had worked with Bonnard on the comedy *L'Albero d'Adamo* (1936). Vergano had also learned how to imbue dramas with elements of sentimentality from his experience on Blasetti's *Sole* as well as Amadeo Nazzari vehicles such as *Quelli della montagna* and *Cavalleria*, two war films in which the protagonists overcome amorous disappointments through heroism on the battlefield.

With its moralistic representation of sexuality unsanctioned by marriage, *Outcry* followed an earlier current in Italian films such as Camerini's *Il Signor Max* (1937), De Sica's *I bambini ci guardano/The Children Are Watching Us* (1943), and *The Gate of Heaven* (1945), Blasetti's *Quattro passi fra le nuvole/Four Steps in the Clouds* (1942), Bonnard's *Campo de' fiori/Peddler and the Lady* (1943), and Visconti's *Ossessione/Obsession* (1943). In these films unsanctioned sex leads directly to personal suffering, a theme that would continue in the postwar and neorealist period. The difference is that in the Italian professional cinema of the 1930s and early 1940s, the *fatalona* indulges in immoral, foreign pastimes that are an expression of anti-Italian culture and threaten the fascist concept of nationhood. For example, in Camerini's *Il Signor Max*, Donna Paolo speaks English, plays bridge, and brags about having visited New York to see the latest Clark Gable movie. She bewitches Gianni, a humble newspaper kiosk owner who pretends to belong to the extranational leisure class in order to court her. In the postwar *Outcry* Matilde's interests in jazz, modern art, and sexual license are no longer threats to the Fascist regime's ideals of Italian national and racial culture, but rather the new standards of virtue in a post-Fascist world based on collective struggle.

Despite this strong moralistic current regarding sexuality, Vergano, like many of his neorealist colleagues in the immediate postwar period, did not limit female displays in *Outcry*.[14] In Vergano's film displays of physicality, alternative sexuality, and hedonism indicate economic selfishness and political arrogance. The lesbian references of the Matilde character in *Outcry* repeat similar themes developed by Rossellini and screenwriter Sergio Amidei in the character of the drug-pushing, lesbian, Nazi agent Ingrid in *Rome Open City*. In *Outcry* the Nazi officer Major Heinrich is equated with the semipagan ideals of physical beauty of Fascist culture. He is introduced doing body-building exercises and vaunting his prowess as a lover. The other German officers, like the upper-class residents of the count's villa, distract themselves with sex and drink. At one point Heinrich even states that he wants a pagan themed party with a pig roast where he can play the part of the sun god Apollo. The equation of hedonism with Fascism and oppression would become a commonplace in cinematic depictions from *Rome Open City* to Liliana Cavani's *Il portiere di notte/The Night Porter* (1974). Pontecorvo would repeat these themes in *Kapò*, in which Edith suffers the humiliation of unsuccessfully trading her virginity to an SS officer for food. In the Pontecorvo film *Burn!* (1969) Walker makes a crude parallel between marriage as slavery and prostitution as wage earning in order to convince the island's sugar barons to abolish slavery on economic rather than on strictly moral grounds.

In contrast, modesty in *Outcry*, as embodied by the traditional female figure Laura, represents the values of self-sacrifice, collectivity, and the solidarity of a reassembled Italian Left. This high moral ground extends to lifestyle differences between rich and poor and is indicative of the ideological influences working within the film. For example, the protagonist Cesare is the son of an overseer who has been able to obtain a middle ground between the working and landowning classes. Cesare is torn between his sense of moral indignation at class inequalities and his father's advice to work in the foundry and accumulate wealth. To emphasize Cesare's dilemma the film constantly shifts between scenes contrasting the opulent landowner's mansion with the humility and poverty of Laura and her comrades. In Matilde's luxurious house, guests listen to music, drink, and dance, in contrast to Laura's spartan room filled with hungry children. The ultimate symbol of the artificial comfort and waste of the upper class is Matilde's greenhouse, which she uses as a *locus amoenus* (love nest) to seduce Cesare. The greenhouse is presented as a place that wastes resources for the pleasure of Matilde, rather than providing needed sustenance for the workers.

Cesare's need to choose between the immediate sexual and financial satisfaction offered by Matilde and the high road of self-sacrifice represented by Laura parallels the decision he must take regarding his political stance in the de facto civil war between Nazis/Fascists and the partisans during the last years of World War II. Vergano's film presents this dilemma in terms of personal and family relationships. Characters like Laura and Matilde offer a parallel between the personal and ideological choices that provide the framework for the entire

film. Pontecorvo would repeat this plot mechanism, whereby a character struggles between short-term advantages and conscience, in many of his later features.
For example, in *Giovanna* (1956), the female protagonist struggles with her husband's opposition to her decision to partake in a textile factory strike. In *La
grande strada azzurra/The Wide Blue Road* (1957), Squarciò must choose between the short-run economic benefits to his family of dynamite fishing and his
responsibility to the fisherman collective. In *Kapò* the deported Jewish girl Edith
must assume the identity of a non-Jewish prisoner in order to survive. In *Burn!*
Walker is torn between his personal loyalty to the rebel leader Josè Dolores and
his own pecuniary interest in quashing the rebellion that Dolores leads.

Pontecorvo's later films attempt to present both sides of a story in a
manner that has much in common with the plot mechanisms in Vergano's
Outcry. In the final scenes of popular revolt and liberation, Matilde stands
recklessly in front of a window exposing herself to the crossfire that results in
her death, a suicide that functions as an attempt to reclaim her honor. Like
Vergano, Pontecorvo emphasizes the human aspect of political decisions to
include choices made by antagonists. For example, in *The Battle of Algiers*
Colonel Mathieu remarks about the irony of fighting a popular resistance,
since his first military experiences were in the anti-Nazi resistance of World
War II. In *Burn!* Walker is torn by his sense of personal and ideological identification with the cause represented by Josè Dolores and his conclusion that
Dolores's goals are impractical and unobtainable.

Another element in Vergano's film that Pontecorvo expanded on is the
idea of a power, even nobility in ignorance. The peasants of the Lombard farms
depicted in *Outcry* live in ignorance and poverty. In *Outcry* this oppression actually forges their ability to express political commitment. Pontecorvo would
rely heavily on this motif in his films, to the point of insisting on the neorealist practice of casting nonprofessional actors whenever possible. For example,
Ali Le Pointe in *The Battle of Algiers* (1966) and Josè Dolores in *Burn!* (1969)
were both played by nonprofessionals, Brahim Haggiag and Evaristo Marquez
respectively, whom Pontecorvo discovered while scouting locations. For *Burn!*
Pontecorvo went to great lengths to oppose studio attempts to cast Sidney
Poitier as Josè Dolores opposite Marlon Brando's Walker. Pontecorvo regret-
tably refused the direction and a writing credit for *Monsieur Klein/Mr. Klein*
(1976) because of the decision to cast French matinee idol Alain Delon in the
starring role.[15] One of Pontecorvo's unfinished projects in the 1980s was a version of the life of Jesus never completed because Pontecorvo, true to his experiences under Vergano and the neorealist school, refused to submit to producer's request to cast a professional actor in the title role.[16]

Pontecorvo's intransigence about nonprofessional actors is actually quite
ironic, since many neorealist films actually made abundant use of professional

actors. The female lead in *Outcry* had first been offered to Clara Calamai, one the most successful professional actresses in the Italian professional cinema of the 1930s and 1940s.[17] The neorealist classic *Rome Open City* featured Anna Magnani and Aldo Fabrizi; both were professional actors and vaudeville stars who had even appeared together in a Mario Bonnard romantic comedy, *Campo de' fiori* (1943). Other neorealist directors were somewhat more rigorous in their use of nonprofessionals during neorealism's heroic period following the war—in films such as De Sica's *Ladri di biciclette/The Bicycle Thief* (1948) and Visconti's *La terra trema/The Earth Trembles* (1948). However, De Sica and Visconti's theatrical experience allowed them to coach nonprofessionals in a manner that often made up for any lack of preparation or experience. The improvisational techniques used by Italian directors working with nonprofessionals are perhaps best demonstrated by Fellini's technique of having actors count aloud instead of reciting lines memorized from a script. The reality of the nonprofessional ideal was that any inconsistency in performance could be fixed in postproduction, since Italian films were often done with postsynchronous sound. Nonprofessionals were simply more malleable to the improvisational approach that neorealist directors favored. Pontecorvo actually began his film career as a nonprofessional actor playing the partisan fighter Pietro in Vergano's *Outcry* (1946). He took this heritage to heart in his legendary confrontations with Marlon Brando on the set of *Burn!* pitting neorealist improvisation against method acting.

Related to this idea of the nobility of ignorance is the depiction of suffering children as a means to elicit emotional reaction. In *Outcry* Laura leads the funeral procession of a child; in another scene a child is killed in crossfire. Vergano also displays the sort of clandestine tactics typical of popular resistance movements that mobilized the least suspect, even children, for a political cause. For example, in *Outcry* the priest asks boys to count the numbers of Nazi soldiers arriving to enforce the occupation. Of course the use of children as an emotional ploy in Italian film was not original to Vergano or the neorealist period. Dependence on innocent characters and children in particular is a continuing characteristic of Italian film from Giovanni Pastrone's *Cabiria* (1914) to Roberto Benigni's *La vita è bella/Life Is Beautiful* (1997). Pontecorvo continued this technique in his films. In *The Wide Blue Road* Squarciò's small sons witness his final agony. In *Kapò* Edith is an innocent girl ignorant of the cruelties and suffering of the world before deportation. Montages of reaction shots of young children abound in *The Battle of Algiers* and especially in *Burn!*—such as the scene in which Josè Dolores holds up a naked infant during a popular celebration of his army's arrival. In *Ogro/Operation Ogre* a young girl recognizes the ETA terrorists as Basques, providing a rare moment of tenderness in the film.

Another neorealist commonplace in Vergano's film, continued by Pontecorvo, is the use of the black market as a backdrop for the presentation of economic issues. In *Outcry*, black market themes are first presented with the character of Cesare's brother Mario, who is hunted down and killed by angry townsfolk when the Fascists begin to lose power. The depiction of Mario's lynching reveals Vergano's debt to Blasetti's interest in Soviet cinema. When Mario is confronted by the townsfolk there is a montage of reactions shots, which include a breast-feeding mother, a group of elderly women, and a farmer on horseback as the representatives of the collective rage that culminates in Mario's death. The theme of black marketeering is also shown from the opposing side when Pietro, played by Pontecorvo, leads the partisans in the theft of trucks and then distributes the stolen flour among the people. Black market themes would appear in Pontecorvo's *The Wide Blue Road* and *Kapò*, among others.

Another key element in Vergano's film later repeated by Pontecorvo is political self-sacrifice and suicide, the negation of or the withdrawal from life in order to satisfy a political aim. In *Outcry* the dual sacrifice of the communist resistance fighter Pietro and the Catholic priest Don Camillo represents the two main forces in the anti-Nazi/Fascist coalition that formed the resistance, another commonplace of neorealism. Vergano even adopts a curious mixture of Christian iconography to portray the sacrifice of the two ideological pillars of the anti-Fascist resistance. Heinrich, the Nazi major, has the prisoners tied to posts and then parades in his jeep as if in a chariot, using their bodies for target practice. The staging recalls martyrdom scenes taken from classical sources reproduced in Enrico Guazzoni's *Quo Vadis?* (1913), remade by Mervyn LeRoy in 1951, in which Christians were martyred in the arena under the eyes of the emperor Nero. The equation of Heinrich with Apollo/Nero and his epicurean wine and sex romps extends to the scene in which Don Camillo and Pietro are captured and the populace gathers to witness their execution. As Don Camillo walks through the crowd to his execution, he leads the surrounding crowd in a crescendo recitation of *Ora pro nobis* until the culminating moment when he and Pietro are shot and fall on top of one another to form a cross, as some critics have noted.[18] Vergano's heavy use of crosscutting and reaction shots again recalls the lessons of Soviet cinema that Vergano learned from Blasetti. By presenting the priest and partisan among a montage of reaction shots of the populace Vergano extends the Catholic imagery of martyrdom to the priest's ideological counterpart, the communist resistance fighter Pietro, played by Pontecorvo.

Plots that elevate heroic self-sacrifice for political ends are a common thread between Vergano and Pontecorvo. Vergano developed this themes in *Pietro Micca* and *Outcry*. Like Vergano's heroes, Pontecorvo's protagonists (Squarciò in *The Wide Blue Road*, Edith in *Kapò*, Ali Le Pointe in

The Battle of Algiers, Josè Dolores in *Burn!*) face their end with a spirit of intransigence and certainty. Before being shot, Pontecorvo's character in *Outcry*, Piero, spits at the Nazi conducting the execution, a sequence that recalls Josè Dolores spitting in Walker's face in *Burn!*

For the depiction of the self-sacrifice of the protagonists in his feature films (Squarciò in *The Wide Blue Road*, Edith in *Kapò*, Ali Le Pointe in *The Battle of Algiers*, and Josè Dolores in *Burn!*), Pontecorvo developed an iconography of lay martyrdom relying heavily on sacred music and Soviet-style choral montages of reaction shots of nonprofessionals. Despite appearances, Pontecorvo's films have references to Catholic themes of sacrifice and redemption, as well as elements that anticipate themes of revolution theology—for instance, in the activism of the character of Don Camillo in *Out-cry*. In *Kapò* Edith enacts a redemptive self-sacrifice that ironically echoes the impulses and the manner of Matilde's suicide in *Outcry*. In *The Battle of Algiers*, after Ali Le Pointe is blown up in his Casbah hiding place, Pontecorvo offers sacred music and images of smoky archways, as if Ali has ascended to a nationalist afterlife. In *Burn!* Walker meets with Josè Dolores and his comrades in a church to make proselytizing arguments about action against the Portuguese. The execution of Josè Dolores amounts to a martyr-dom that repeats the imagery of popular reaction from the execution of Pietro and Don Camillo in *Outcry*. In *Ogro* Francoist minister Carrero Blanco's daily routine of attending mass allows the ETA Basques to organ-ize his assassination.

Pontecorvo's later feature films have too much in common with Vergano's *Outcry* for the connection to be casual.[19] His appearance as the re-sistance martyr Pietro, as well as the roles played by future directors Carlo Lizzani and Giuseppe De Santis, may have originally been because the film's ex-partisan producers lacked funds to hire professional actors. However, the style and thematic elements of *Outcry* resonate so deeply and repeatedly in Pontecorvo's later features that Vergano must be considered as a profound in-fluence on Pontecorvo. Pontecorvo's participation in *Outcry* seems to be the germ, the foundation, the source of the cinematic vision that he transferred to the historical settings in his films: the Holocaust in *Kapò*, the Algerian revolt against France in *The Battle of Algiers*, the colonial and postcolonial process in *Burn!* and the Basque terrorist movement in *Ogro*.

NOTES

1. Carlo Celli, "Aldo Vergano's *Il sole sorge ancora/Outcry* (1946) as Influence on Gillo Pontecorvo," *Forum Italicum* 38, no. 1 (Spring 2004): 217–28.

2. Luigi Cipriani, M. Conciatori, M. Giraldi, and L. Ricci, eds., *Primo piano sull'autore Gillo Pontecorvo "La dittatura della verità"* (Rome: Designer, 1999), 22.

3. Franca Faldini and Goffredo Fofi, eds., *L'Avventurosa storia del cinema Italian raccontata dai suoi protagonisti, 1935–1959* (Milan: Feltrinelli, 1979), 120.

4. Faldini and Fofi, *L'Avventurosa*, 119.

5. Faldini and Fofi, *L'Avventurosa*, 24. See also Aldo Vergano, *Cronaca degli anni perduti: Memorie* (Firenze, Italy: Parenti, 1958).

6. See Adriano Aprà and Riccardo Redi, eds., *Sole: Soggetto, sceneggiatura, note per la realizzazione* (Rome: Di Giacomo, 1985).

7. See Paola Micheli, *Il cinema di Blasetti, Parlò così* (Rome: Bulzoni Editore, 1990); Alessandro Blasetti, *Il cinema che ho vissuto,* ed. Franco Prono (Bari, Italy: Edizioni dedalo, 1982); Gianfranco Gori, *Alessandro Blasetti* (Firenze, Italy: La Nuova Italia, 1984); Luca Verdone, *Il film di Alessandro Blasetti* (Rome: Gremese, 1989).

8. In fact it was Vergano who first introduced Rossellini and Amidei; Faldini and Fofi, *L'Avventurosa*, 48.

9. For a discussion of the relationship between the Italian professional cinema of the 1930s and 1940s and neorealism see Carlo Celli, "The Legacy of the Films of Mario Camerini in Vittorio De Sica's *Ladri di biciclette/The Bicycle Thief* (1948)," *Cinema Journal* 40, no. 4 (2001): 3–17; "Alessandro Blasetti and Representations of Italian Fascism in the 1930s," *Italian Culture* 16, no. 2 (1998): 99–109; "Italian Neorealism's Wartime Legacy: Roberto Rossellini's *Rome Open City* and *Man of the Cross*," *Romance Languages Annual* 10 (1998): 225–28.

10. Roberto Chiti and Enrico Lancia, *Dizionario del cinema italiano: I Film vol. 1, dal 1930 al 1944* (Rome: Gremese, 1993), 14.

11. See Carlo Celli, "A Lost De Sica Film—*La porta del cielo/The Gate of Heaven* (1945)," *Quarterly Review of Film and Video* 18, no. 4, 361–70.

12. Faldini and Fofi, *L'Avventurosa*, 120.

13. The term *telefono bianco* (white telephone) refers to the tendency of Italian romantic comedies of the 1930s to feature a scene in an upscale dwelling in which a character speaks on a white, enameled telephone.

14. A facile explanation for the popularity of neorealist films outside of Italy is the extension of realism to the depiction of the female form, including the bodies of actresses such as Silvana Mangano in *Riso amaro* (*Bitter Rice*, 1949) and even Ingrid Bergman in *Stromboli—Terra di Dio* (*Stromboli*, 1949). See Gregory D. Black, *The Catholic Crusade against the Movies, 1940–1975* (Cambridge: Cambridge University Press, 1997); and Mary Ann Doane, *The Desire to Desire: The Woman's Film of the 1940's* (Bloomington: Indiana University Press, 1987).

15. Alessandro Levantesi, "Intervista," in Cipriani, Conciatori, Giraldi, and Ricci, *Primo piano*, 29.

16. See Irene Bignardi, *Memorie estorte a uno smemorato vita di Gillo Pontecorvo* (Milan: Feltrinelli, 1999).

17. Faldini and Fofi, *L'Avventurosa*, 119.

18. Paolo Mereghetti, *Il Mereghetti dizionario dei film 2000* (Milan: Baldini and Castoldi, 1999), 1701.

19. Bignardi, *Memorie*, 69.

The Neorealist Tradition and Pontecorvo's Early Documentaries, 1953–1956

$\mathcal{W}$hen Pontecorvo was fresh from his experiences in the World War II resistance, the Italian film industry was in difficult period. In 1948 just over fifty films were made in Italy. The Italian film industry entered a difficult period, with low production hampering profits and future production. In July 1949 the Italian government took steps to encourage a previously vibrant national film industry by passing legislation that granted reduction of taxes for a film of Italian origin. This law took effect in 1950 and remained until 1955. In 1956 it was replaced by a law that raised the number of days per year Italian theaters were required to book Italian films from eighty to one hundred.[1] However, government patronage came with strings attached in the form of the reticence of the Christian Democrat coalition government to support films depicting social problems. The subsidies for Italian film production, including shorts and documentaries, were dependent on a standard of "artistic and technical merits" to be determined by government officials. The arrangement became known as the "Andreotti law," named after long-serving cabinet minister Giulio Andreotti. Andreotti reacted negatively to the films of Vittorio De Sica, like *Ladri di biciclette/The Bicycle Thief* (1948) and *Umberto D.* (1952), which he felt depicted Italy in a negative light.[2]

Part of the Italian government's efforts to promote the domestic film industry was a requirement that theaters show a short documentary, often made with government funding, before a feature. One famous example is Antonioni's *Nettezza urbana/N.U.* (1948). These government grants allowed Pontecorvo to become a professional director. Pontecorvo's early documentaries reveal unequivocally that his cinematic origins are in the neorealist style. In his documentaries Pontecorvo solidified the influences he received in the heady postwar period as an actor on Aldo Vergano's *Il sole sorge ancora/Outcry*. Pontecorvo's insistence on being able to cast nonprofessional actors in settings that were not artificially created and his insistence on story lines with a progressive political element were all confirmed during his period as a neorealist documentarian before 1957.

LA MISSIONE TIMIRIAZEV/THE TIMIRIAZEV MISSION (1953)

Pontecorvo's first documentary film, *La Missione Timiriazev/The Timiriazev Mission* (1953) has a style that recalls Soviet propaganda films, which must have pleased the communist labor union, the CGIL, that financed the film. *The Timiriazev Mission* was shot on sixteen and thirty-five millimeter film and opens with intertexts describing floods in the Polesine region of the Po River valley in 1951 and the aid received from the Soviet Union in the aftermath. The film has little of the narrative characterizations that would be a staple of Pontecorvo's later films, although Pontecorvo would start most of his later feature films with a similar voice-over or documentary-style introduction. In *The Timiriazev Mission* Pontecorvo displays an knack for filming crowd scenes, an ability that he would use again in the intricately staged crowd scenes of later films like *La battaglia di Algeri/The Battle of Algiers* and *Queimada!/Burn!* If the film has a narrative tract it is in the sense of proletarian solidarity and collective identity forged by the catastrophe of the flood. Thus the flood is presented not only as a natural calamity but as an opportunity for Italians to express a political culture in accordance with the views of the producers of the film.

In the autumn of 1951 a flood struck in the Po valley region of Northern Italy. Pontecorvo shows a montage of rushing water in typical newsreel style with mounting musical accompaniment. The flooding had effects across much of the Italian peninsula, and the narrator begins a roll call accompanied by images of communes hit particularly hard in the rural regions near the cities of Pavia and Rovigo. The narrator lists the number of deaths with images of dead cattle and desperate women and children, with a voice-over chronicle of attempts at evacuation and reconstruction that emphasizes the importance of the collective struggle against natural calamity. Pontecorvo accompanies these comments with shots of people crowding the banks waiting for the water to recede. The film emphasizes the heroic efforts of the local left-wing worker organizations, the *camere del lavoro* (work cooperatives), as well as the many truckers, dock workers, and fishermen who assisted in the evacuation and care of refugees. The voice-over details nighttime spotlight searches for survivors on the flooded river and the dedication of workers who reinforced dykes at night. The film develops these themes with shots of boats being loaded with supplies, people being taken to safety, and repeated mention of the heroic proletarian organizations whose teams of volunteers manned the refugee centers shown in the documentary.

After the opening emphasizing the efforts of Italian workers at the outset of the flood, the film concentrates on rebuilding efforts and the arrival of aid from the Soviet Union. A shot of the Cyrillic text of a Russian newspaper headline announces the arrival of Russian aid, accompanied by the strains of the Soviet anthem and images of a flying red flag. The narrator announces that the Russian cargo ship *Timiriazev* arrived from Odessa in record time, giving the film its title. The port of Genoa greets the ship with horns and twirling cranes in a celebratory montage accompanied by the Soviet anthem and a heroic voice-over about Soviet worker associations coming to the aid of their Italian comrades. Pontecorvo offers scenes of Italian labor union leaders greeting the Soviets, as the film dutifully reports the names of the Italian functionaries and the Soviet ambassadors who give speeches to a crowd assembled on the Genoa docks. The film shifts to a map that details visits by a Soviet delegation, alternating with stills of happy Italian townsfolk greeting their Soviet benefactors. As the Soviets depart by train, shots of waving crowds are accompanied by Beethoven's Ninth Symphony and followed by stills of the Soviet delegation's visit to southern Italy. Pontecorvo's documentary then recounts that the workers in Genoa unloaded the boat without accepting pay, in scenes that include an attempt at more personal characterizations. Actually the most evocative moment of the film is when an Italian worker whistles a workers' song and is joined by a Russian sailor. They sing together before the unloading of a threshing machine, trucks, and tractors donated by the Russians, who leave the assembly area to the flag-waving workers. The film ends with platitudes about unity and peace and a last shot of the red flag as the ship departs after having heroically completed its mission.

The flood took place at the height of the Cold War, in 1951—before Stalin's death in 1954, before Kruschev's secret speech to the Russian Communist Party admitting to Stalin's purges and crimes, and before Pontecorvo left the Italian Communist Party in 1956 (following the Soviet Union's military repression of the prodemocracy revolts in Hungary). *The Timiriazev Mission* gives an indication of the prestige that the Soviet Union enjoyed among members of the Italian Left in the early postwar period. It was a time when Soviet dictator Joseph Stalin was known as Uncle Joe (*Baffone* in Italy), the leader who had helped to liberate Europe rather than enslave it under communist totalitarianism. Of course, aid to the victims of the Polesine flooding actually arrived from many countries. The film emphasizes the political ties between the Soviet Union and the Italian Communist Party. The reason for the flood was an unfortunate combination of heavy rains, high sea level, erosion, overbuilding, and deforestation. None of these factors are mentioned, as the film displays an interesting lack of environmental awareness, which, like the uncritical presentation of the Soviet Union, was part of the political culture of the time in some sectors.

CANI DIETRO LE SBARRE/DOGS BEHIND BARS (1954)

Common settings of neorealist documentaries were the peripheries of Italian cities, which after the war struggled from an influx of new inhabitants and were bubbling with black market economic activity. Pontecorvo, like many filmmakers of the neorealist period, set documentaries in these locations. He was attracted by the intermingling of people at the humblest social levels, which offered a contrast between the genuine impulses of the inhabitants and the austere, impersonal, and often dysfunctional architecture of concrete slab, high-rise apartment buildings in the Le Corbusier or Gropius style.[3] Pontecorvo's documentary *Cani dietro le sbarre/Dogs behind Bars* (1954) opens with sweeping pans of these urban dwellings and concentrates on the struggle between dogcatchers and their prey. Pontecorvo reportedly used his abilities from his days in the underground in order to gain the confidence of the dogcatchers, posing as a journalist doing a report on dangerous strays.[4] The stories behind the making of the film give an indication of the simple, improvisational essence of the neorealist style. The off-camera narration is accompanied by whistled tune and piano, reportedly authored by Pontecorvo, which betrays his interest in and ability to compose simple melodies. When Pontecorvo's troupe lost part of the sound track, Pontecorvo reportedly imitated the barking of dogs needed for the final mix.[5] The assistant director and composer of the narration, Fausta Leoni, would collaborate with Pontecorvo on his project on magic and the paranormal in the late 1960s.

The film has a certain rhythm that would mark Pontecorvo's later works. He uses long establishing shots of the locations and then switches to montages of more personal, individual events, in this case of dogs being caught, or of people trying to help the dogs escape from the dogcatchers. The film has a keen eye for neorealist aesthetics. There are close-ups of dogcatchers whose faces recall the visage of Lamberto Maggiorani, the nonprofessional star of De Sica's *The Bicycle Thief*. Pontecorvo's allegiances in the film are clearly with the poor strays that are rounded up and brought to a municipal dog pound. The film follows their destiny from the street to the dogcatcher's truck to the dog pound, where they are allowed four days for adoption before being gassed. Pontecorvo follows all of these steps clinically and demonstrates great strength as a filmmaker able to depict all sides of a story. His close-ups of depressed dogs awaiting execution are eloquent in their desperation. But Pontecorvo also explains the necessity for municipal dogcatchers. The narrator lists the number of people bitten by dogs daily in Rome and explains the difficulties and dangers of the dog-catching profession. The film has another neorealist constant, which is perhaps merely an expression of the demographic reality of postwar Italy, in the scenes with children who root for the dogs to escape or cry when a dog has been caught and they cannot afford to free it from the kennel. The film ends after scenes alluding to (not showing) dogs being gassed and showing a man who adopts a dog on the day it was to be gassed. Unlike in *The Timiriazev Mission*, in *Dogs behind Bars* Pontecorvo displays a clear adhesion to the neorealist style of filmmaking and a sense of narrative emanating from the *versimo* (naturalism) literary school of the late nineteenth century. Pontecorvo's film tries to present all sides of the story: the efforts of the dogcatchers to keep the city safe from strays, the desperation and suffering of the unfortunate dogs that are captured and gassed, the luck of a dog who is saved by an act of generosity, and above all the reactions of the people in the Roman periphery.

Several of Pontecorvo's other documentaries have clear echoes of the neorealist style. *Porta portese/Portese Gate* (1954), apparently Pontecorvo's favorite of his documentaries, is set at the huge open-air marketplace at Porta Portese in Rome, a location also featured in an important sequence of De Sica's *The Bicycle Thief*. Pontecorvo's documentary includes a small cameo of a young pregnant woman passing though the stalls at the marketplace with her husband. Pontecorvo focuses on this pair as they look at the objects on display beyond their means.[6] Like his neorealist colleagues, Pontecorvo appreciated the natural expressions and realism of nonprofessional actors. The episode, with its setting and concentration on the theme of a desire for consumer objects, seems to be taken from filmmaking theories by Cesare Zavattini. Zavattini, De Sica's screenwriter on *The Bicycle Thief*, emphasized the eloquence of everyday life and its ability to convey a larger social reality in film.[7] Pontecorvo would repeat these techniques in other documentaries, such as *Festa a Castelluccio/Festival at Castelluccio* (1955), set in a small town of Norcia that celebrates the end of winter with a town festival, and *Uomini di marmo/Men of Marble* (1955), a short documentary about the marble quarries of Apuane.[8]

PANE E ZOLFO/BREAD AND SULFUR (1956)

Pane e zolfo/Bread and Sulfur, one of Pontecorvo's last documentaries before he became a feature film director, is set in the town of Ca' Bernardi in the

Marches region of Italy. The film begins by recounting the story of the occupation of a mine slated for closing, a topic also examined in Pietro Germi's Italian emigration drama, *Il cammino della speranza/ The Road of Hope* (1950). *Bread and Sulfur* opens with a shot of three smiling but dirty miners that cuts to an establishing shot of the hills of the Marches over the sulfur deposits. The composition follows the format typical of government-subsidized films of the period, with a still shot of miners framing their experience within the geography of the working experience. The voice-over narration introduces themes of the decline of the mines and the economic repercussions on the local populace. Shots of the decrepit and abandoned mines are intercut with images of abandoned towns. The narrator makes the point that when eighteen hundred miners lost their jobs those firings had a devastating effect on eighteen hundred families.

Like Pontecorvo's first documentary, *The Timiriazev Mission*, *Bread and Sulfur* seems to open with the tone of a propaganda film. But *Bread and Sulfur* does not display the heavy-handed rhetoric of *The Timiriazev Mission* and instead repeats the more personal narratives developed in *Dogs behind Bars*. True to the style of neorealist filmmaking, *Bread and Sulfur* allows the images to speak for themselves. Pontecorvo's film scans the fronts of the abandoned houses with a subjective camera that weaves details of everyday life in towns where the mines have closed into narrative elements that are more effective than the propagandistic tones of Pontecorvo's first film. *Bread and Sulfur* offers shots of displaced workers stealing bricks from the abandoned factory. Elderly inhabitants collect chicory in order to supplement their diets. A female letter carrier is mobbed by townspeople eager for letters from the numerous townspeople who have emigrated. The film has images of young women dancing with one another, an eloquent comment on the lack of young men in a town where the youth must leave in order to create a future. When the narrator finally comments that these formerly vibrant towns have become the abode of the old, the infirm, and anyone else who cannot leave, the images have already conveyed the message without any need for rhetorical embellishment.

The film would anticipate fears about mining disasters, as it was made very close to the occurrence of a mining disaster in Marcinelle, Belgium (1956), which claimed the lives of many Italian emigrants. The theme of closed mines and suffering workers was emotionally charged at the time. This point is emphasized in an interview with a trigenerational mining family, with the narrator speaking in the voice of a middle-aged man sitting between his father and son. The man describes the last attempt by the workers to occupy the mine, a common tactic by striking workers in the 1950s. Part of the strategy of unions of the period was to occupy the means of production and continue working in order to demonstrate their goodwill. Pontecorvo offers newsreel footage of the strike, with images of townspeople collecting supplies for the miners after their forty-first day below ground and a crowd of family members waiting at the mine entrance in hopes of news about the negotiations. As the film shifts to documentary footage of the strike, the film returns to the straight documentary formalism of *The Timiriazev Mission* with a montage of women throwing flowers to the striking miners although as the film points out ultimately the efforts of the strikers had little effect. In his early documentaries Pontecorvo demonstrates two key influences that would dominate his future efforts as a feature filmmaker. Firstly Pontecorvo has a fondness for the rhetoric of the political Left. Pontecorvo was heavily influenced by the comrades of his brother Bruno Pontecorvo, the physicist who defected to the Soviet Union in order to work on the Soviet nuclear weapons program. Pontecorvo was also a resistance leader in northern Italy working with future leaders of the Italian Communist Party during World War II. Pontecorvo's first documentary, *The Timiriazev Mission*, parrots the style of Soviet propaganda films with heroic voice-overs, martial music, and images of red, hammer-and-sickled flags waving in the wind. Pontecorvo's subsequent documentaries, like *Bread and Sulfur* and *Dogs behind Bars*, demonstrate a second, but key, ability: adherence to the powerful imagery and narrative simplicity of Italian neorealism. *Bread and Sulfur* and *Dogs behind Bars* allow the images of the subject to communicate the reality at hand; they have an interest in personal stories that eloquently describe economic and political situations. When Pontecorvo shows people stealing bricks and the deserted cityscape of a town whose inhabitants have been forced to emigrate due to a mine closing, there is little need for flag-waving rhetoric, and the communicative impact of the film is far greater.

NOTES

1. Gianfranco Casadio, *Il grigio e il nero: Spettacolo e propaganda nel cinema italiano degli anni trenta (1931–1943)* (Ravenna, Italy: Longo, 1989), 16. For a synopsis of the economic and political history of Italian cinema see Gian Piero Brunetta, *Guida alla storia del cinema italiano, 1905–2003* (Turin: Einaudi, 2003), 425–47.

2. Marga Cottino-Jones, *A Student's Guide to Italian Cinema*, 2nd ed. (Dubuque, IA: Kendall Hunt, 1992).

3. Irene Bignardi, *Memorie estorte a uno smemorato vita di Gillo Pontecorvo* (Milan: Feltrinelli, 1999), 76.

4. Bignardi, *Memorie*, 76.

5. Bignardi, *Memorie*, 76.

6. Bignardi, *Memorie*, 77.

7. See Cesare Zavattini, *Opere, 1931–1986* (Milan: Bompiani, 1991).

8. Simone Emiliani, "Dai documentari ai cortometraggi," in *Primo piano sull'autore Gillo Pontecorvo: "La dittatura della verità,"* ed. Luigi Cipriani, M. Conciatori, M. Giraldi, and L. Ricci (Rome: Designer, 1999), 100.

First Features: *Giovanna* (1956) and *La grande strada azzurra/ The Wide Blue Road* (1957)

GIOVANNA (1956)

Giovanna (1956) is an episodic film that was funded by the Woman's International Democratic Federation of the East German communist government (DDR) in Joris Ivens' collection of short films on women's issues titled *Die Winderose/Rose of the Winds* (1956). The film features contributions from directors around the world. The Brazilian episode, by Alex Viany, is about a woman farm worker. The Russian episode, by Sergei Gerassimov, is about a girl on a collective farm who goes to start another farm. *Giovanna*, the Italian episode directed by Pontecorvo, depicts a women's strike at a textile factory. For *Giovanna*, Pontecorvo was able to gather key members of the troupe that he would use on his later features, including screenwriter Franco Solinas and assistant director Giuliano Montaldo. The French episode in *Rose of the Winds*, by Yannick Bellon, is about a teacher played by Simone Signoret. The Chinese episode, by Wu Kuo-Yin, is about village cooperatives. The episode about a collective farm by Gerassimov reportedly did not please the Russian authorities, who had provided most of the financing for the film, so that *Rose of the Winds* actually had difficulty finding distributors.[1] The film was apparently never commercially released in Italy, although Pontecorvo's contribution, *Giovanna*, was presented at the Venice Film Festival.

Given the fact that the film was largely funded by monies from the communist Eastern Bloc, Pontecorvo's contribution, *Giovanna*, would seem to run the danger of sharing the rhetorical excesses of his first documentary, *The Timiriazev Mission*, about Soviet aid to the flooded Po valley. On the surface a story about a women's strike in an Italian textile mill offers a perfect opportunity for the sort of flag-waving rhetoric used in *La Missione Timiriazev/*

The Timiriazev Mission. Given the actual backdrop behind the propagandistic presentation of some the episodes—such as the Soviet forced starvation of Ukrainian farmers or the murderous course of the collectivization drives during Mao Tse-tung's subsequent cultural revolution in China—*Rose of the Winds* portrays the hyperbolic idealism that pervaded the international communist movement during the Cold War.[2] However, instead of using the rhetoric of *The Timiriazev Mission*, Pontecorvo's episode, *Giovanna*, evidences the lessons that Pontecorvo gained from his experience directing *Cani dietro le sbarre/Dogs behind Bars* and *Pane e zolfo//Bread and Sulfur* and his mastery of the Italian neorealist documentary style.

The film opens as the protagonist, Giovanna, argues with her husband about whether she will go to work or take care of their infant. The protagonist is played by Armida Gianassi, a nonprofessional actress Pontecorvo found one afternoon at a local dancing club.[3] The argument between husband and wife in the opening sequence gives the film a feminist tone ahead of its time. Giovanna's husband does not approve of his wife's having a job and is further annoyed that she is considering participating in a strike. Pontecorvo's film goes from the microcosm of familial discussion to larger issues of class conflict when a car carrying the factory manager arrives with a list of workers to be fired. A pregnant worker faints at the news she has been laid off, provoking an emotional reaction from the rest of the workers, sparking the occupation of the factory.

Pontecorvo presents the struggle of the striking women as emblematic of the struggle between collective and individual consciousness, a theme he would repeat in his later features. The ability of the women to sacrifice for the collective good of all the workers is developed through attention to details about family responsibility, repeating the theme from the opening sequences of the film. Husbands waiting outside the factory gates use megaphones to speak to their striking wives. These megaphone sequences, with the women singing to their husbands and the outside world, recall Giuseppe De Santis's portrayal of the *mondine* (rice pickers) in *Riso amaro/Bitter Rice* (1948), another film with the theme of individual versus collective values. Pontecorvo would also repeat the narrative tension created among a group of segregated females in his later film *Kapò* (1959).

Pontecorvo indicates the passage of time through montages of men struggling with domestic chores and the establishment of a food drive to support the families of striking workers. These scenes of community solidarity are intercut with shots of women emblematically behind barred windows in the factory, with a voice-over explaining police attempts to contain the strike, such as the closing of the road and cutting of electrical power. Part of the tactics of striking workers during the period was to occupy factories and continue to work as a sign of goodwill. Pontecorvo's film emphasizes the solidarity of workers and their efforts to continue working. But after the electric power has been cut off for twenty-five days of the strike tensions mount. The town storekeeper refuses to extend credit to the families of striking workers. Divisions between the strikers increase, and the head of the strike feels forced to reveal the names of the workers who have been slated for dismissal by management. The film's protagonist, Giovanna, calms tensions by convincing the electricity workers union to hook up an illegal power line, a demonstration of proletarian solidarity—which is key in Pontecorvo's political outlook. However, the factory manager announces that the first eighty-five striking workers who present themselves for work will have their jobs back. Once a single mother of four accepts the owner's terms and decides to reclaim her job, the strike breaks. The film ends with a voice-over about the moral victory of the strikers, who occupied the factory for thirty-five days.

The film displays stylistic elements that Pontecorvo gained from Soviet formalism, which had been a large influence not only on neorealism but also on the Italian professional cinema of the 1930s. Pontecorvo communicates the drama of events with a flurry of reaction shots in a formalist style, with stark natural lighting and montage of low-angle shots. This composition renders the striking workers more noble. Crane shots within the factory setting portray the oppressive nature of the setting. The film's subject matter and its characterizations also seem to owe a great deal to Pontecorvo's experiences on the set of Aldo Vergano's *Il sole sorge ancora/Outcry*. The emphasis on collective action, the style of reaction shots, and the heroic portrayal of a struggle of good versus evil echo the themes and style of Vergano's film. *Giovanna* is an early example of Pontecorvo's ability to arrive at narrative essence and character development in a few quick shots. This sense of urgency in characterization is one of the basic traits of the neorealist style and of Pontecorvo's other cinematic model, Rossellini's *Paisà*. Importantly, *Giovanna* does not have the overbearing rhetoric that characterized Pontecorvo's first film, *The Timiriazev Mission*. Interestingly, *Giovanna* is actually one of the few films by Pontecorvo with a happy ending.[4] His characters realize their goals, as the factory owner's attempt to divide the workers is unsuccessful.

With *Giovanna*, Pontecorvo debuted in the Italian cinema industry as the neorealist period was reaching its end. When Pontecorvo made *Giovanna*, Antonioni was shooting the psychological study *Le amiche/The Girlfriends* (1955), Fellini was making *Il bidone/The Swindler* (1955), Visconti had made the historically removed love tragedy *Senso/The Wanton Countess*, and De Sica was planning what would be, arguably, the last neorealist feature film, *Il tetto/The Roof* (1957).[5] Thus, given its connection to the history of neorealism, *Giovanna* seems like a return to an earlier era.[6] The film recalls Pontecorvo's documentaries, with somber voice-overs and melancholy accordion music and scenes of

Yves Montand (Squariciò) and Alida Valli (Rosetta) in The Wide Blue Road.
Courtesy of Milestone Films

desperate women dancing in a courtyard, as in *Bread and Sulfur*. *Giovanna* is imbued with the themes, again prevalent in Pontecorvo's earlier documentaries, of solidarity against oppression and collective action versus individual initiative. Ultimately the film seems to mix elements of a feature film and a documentary short. Actually, despite directing big-budget productions in his later career, including the United Artists–financed *Queimada!/Burn!* (1969), Pontecorvo never truly progressed beyond the thematic essence of this stark neorealist documentary style of filmmaking. The narrator voice-overs and documentary style in *Giovanna* reappear in some form in all of his feature films.

LA GRANDE STRADA AZZURRA/THE WIDE BLUE ROAD (1957)

After his contribution of *Giovanna* for Joris Ivens's episodic film *Rose of the Winds*, Pontecorvo was approached to direct a feature-length film to be based on *Squarciò* (*Squarciò the Fisherman*), a novella about a Sardinian dynamite fisherman written by Franco Solinas, Pontecorvo's writing partner on *Giovanna*. Collaboration with Solinas would be central to Pontecorvo's career, as the only feature that Pontecorvo made without Solinas was his last film, *Ogro/Operation Ogre* (1979). Yet Pontecorvo reportedly hesitated before accepting the assignment to direct *La grande strada azzurra/The Wide Blue Road* because the film's producers demanded stylistic concessions that meant a break with the neorealist style he used for *Giovanna*. Pontecorvo's cast would include professional actors, including the Franco-Italian film and cabaret star Yves Montand, in a role that critics felt recalled his appearance as a money-hungry truck driver in Henri-Georges Clouzot's *The Wages of Fear* (1953), as well as Alida Valli, an actress whose international reputation had been solidified by her starring roles in Carol Reed's *The Third Man* (1949) and Luchino Visconti's *Senso/The Wanton Countess* (1954). Pontecorvo initially objected to the producers' insistence that the film be in color, even though he had experimented with color film in his documentary about Roman dogcatchers. *Dogs behind Bars. The Wide Blue Road* is an example of what has become known as "pink neorealism," a term to describe Italian films in the 1950s that retained some of the narrative essence of the neorealist period, but made concessions to what producers anticipated that audiences would prefer, such as recognizable stars and color film. Pontecorvo was eventually persuaded to accept the project, because directing *The Wide Blue Road* meant entry into the film industry as a true feature film director.

Pontecorvo was not the only director with a past in neorealism to make concessions to audience and producer demands. By the 1950s Italian films had begun to abandon wartime themes and focus on the energy of the next generation. Despite film historians' dramatizations of the crisis of neorealism that erupted at the 1954 Venice Film Festival, pitting supporters of Fellini's *La Strada* (1954) against supporters of Visconti's *The Wanton Countess* (1954), the actual content of Italian cinema in the 1950s was not dramatically different from its content in the 1930s and even the silent period. Italian production in the 1950s was dominated by costume dramas, peplum, melodrama, and comedies, with a new role call of leading men and physically attractive ladies.[7] Even ideologically rigid directors like De Santis, who would remain in the Italian Communist Party despite the invasion of Hungary in 1956, contributed to this return of spectacle to the Italian cinema. The star of De Santis's film *Bitter Rice* (1948), Silvana Mangano, communicated the attraction of cartoon pinups or female figures painted on the fuselage of American B-29 bombers, as well as De Santis's collectivist message. Pontecorvo's *The Wide Blue Road* also has a nod to the *maggiorata fisiche* (buxom lady) figure—made popular in Italian film through the efforts of beauty pageant contestants turned actresses such as Sophia Loren and Gina Lollobrigida—with the appearance of Federica Ranchi, who displays her legs in the surf in her role as Squarciò's daughter. When Pontecorvo debuted as a feature film director he entered a film industry that was actively seeking and gaining audience approval. In fact, the Italian film industry in the mid-1950s was working to increase its market share and was positioning itself for the early 1960s, during which Italian production was second only to that of Hollywood. When Pontecorvo debuted as a director with *The Wide Blue Road*, the early period of heroic, progressively themed, neorealist dramas, filmed in black and white with nonprofessional actors, had seen its best days.

In making *The Wide Blue Road* Pontecorvo may have been upset about the style of film he had to complete, but he had no compunctions about the story, based on a novel by Franco Solinas about a stubborn Sardinian fisherman. Solinas's novel *Squarciò the Fisherman* recalls Giovanni Verga's novel about Sicilian fishermen, *I Malavoglia/The House by the Meddlar Tree*, later adapted for the screen by Luchino Visconti as the canonical neorealist film *La terra trema/The Earth Trembles* (1948). Visconti was one of the founding fathers of the neorealist style, with his film *Ossessione/Obsession* (1943) based on James Cain's novel *The Postman Always Rings Twice*.[8] Like Visconti's *The Earth Trembles*, Pontecorvo's *The Wide Blue Road* is essentially a melodramatic story about a family's attempt to raise its economic station. However, in Visconti's film the protagonists work collectively, whereas in *The Wide Blue Road* the protagonist, Squarciò, is an antagonist to collective values.

As the film opens it is evident that Pontecorvo approached the direction of his first full-length feature film with stylistic strategies from his early documentaries. Like *Bread and Sulfur* or *Giovanna*, *The Wide Blue Road* opens with a voice-over of platitudes about land, sea, and family ties, as if Pontecorvo were making another documentary. The first sequence features Squarciò plying his trade, dismantling artillery shells and packing gunpowder into bombs that he will use to kill fish.[9] When Squarciò arrives at port with his catch of prize fish, he is criticized by fishermen who accuse him of ruining the ecological integrity of the sea beds by blowing up the water and the fish. Although the film was made in the mid-1950s, an era of limited environmental awareness, it was already common knowledge that dynamite fishing destroys the ecological balances that allow fish to breed. In the film the fishermen openly resent Squarciò's methods. Squarciò attempts to keep the peace by claiming that he sets off his bombs only in remote areas and, perhaps more importantly, that he does not sell the village wholesaler his catch of larger fish unless the wholesaler has accepted the catch of the other fishermen. These opening scenes seem taken directly from the opening sequences of Visconti's *The Earth Trembles*, which depicts Sicilian fishermen haggling unsuccessfully with wholesalers.

Despite this opening display of solidarity with the other fishermen, Squarciò's instincts are entirely individualistic. He refuses the invitation of his childhood friend Salvatore to contribute to the purchase of a refrigerator so that the fishermen's cooperative may eliminate the wholesaler. When Squarciò realizes that the coast guard has a fast boat, he buys a motor fast enough to outrun the authorities. He signs promissory notes to buy the motor in another scene that seems taken straight from Verga's novel *The House by the Meddlar Tree* and Visconti's adaptation of it, *La terra trema/The Earth Trembles*. Squarciò is forced to sink the boat and the new motor when the coast guard nearly catches him dynamite fishing. Squarciò later breaks the fishermen's code by buying the boat of Santamaria (the estranged father of his childhood friend Salvatore) at auction with money borrowed from the fish wholesaler. According to the local code of conduct, the collective of fishermen should have allowed Santamaria's family to reclaim the confiscated property at a lower price.

Part of the collective underpinning of the film is the strong patriarchal culture of the fishermen. Squarciò, the dynamite fisherman played by Yves Montand, is the undisputed head of his nuclear family. The patriarchal order extends to the younger male members of his family when it comes to preserving the honor of the females in the family. When Tonino, Squarciò's adolescent son, catches his nubile sister Diana and Domenico kissing on the beach, the couple insist that they will marry in response to the child's insistence that family honor be respected. Squarciò justifies his individualistic actions as part of his duty to retain his role as family patriarch. But his inability to adapt these instincts to the opportunity offered by the fishermen's cooperative eventually causes his downfall.

Squarciò's ostracism from the collective group of fishermen comes to a climax when he dares to attend the village dance celebrating the new fishermen's cooperative. Squarciò decides to reconcile with his childhood friend Salvatore, since their children, Diana and Renato, wish to marry. But the reconciliation is based on personal issues and will not extend to Squarciò's profession. When Squarciò affirms his decision to continue dynamite fishing, he is viewed with diffidence by his own young sons Tonino and Bore, who remain unconvinced of his individualistic methods. They try to dissuade him from dynamite fishing from the shore now that he has sunk his boat in order to avoid the coast guard. The boys reluctantly accompany their father in the last sequence in the film, in which Squarciò mortally wounds himself and injures his eldest son, Tonino, when a bomb explodes unexpectedly. The film ends as Squarciò's smallest son, Bore, rows his injured brother back to their pregnant mother, Rosetta, leaving a penitent and mortally wounded Squarciò at the site of his fatal bomb blast. Thus, in *The Wide Blue Road* Squarciò's individualistic attempts to enrich himself and his rejection of the benefits of the collective of fishermen end in defeat.

Squarciò's efforts to deny the moral and economic validity of collective action injure not only himself but all those who copy his methods. There is a brief love story between Squarciò's daughter Diana and Domenico, a quarry worker who initially refuses to sell explosives to Squarciò. Domenico changes his mind once the quarry is set to close and he must find a source of income in order to marry Diana. But, like Squarciò, Domenico is punished for his initiative; he is mortally wounded when he drops dynamite he intended to sell to Squarciò in an attempt to flee from Gaspare, another of Squarciò's boyhood friends, now a coast guard officer. The aftermath of Domenico's death in turn causes Gaspare to quit his job. It may be argued that as a policeman, in terms of Pontecorvo's political views, Gaspare represents and defends the interests of the wholesaler and the continental fishing concerns. Yet Gaspare, like Domenico, is ultimately a victim of Squarciò's individualistic impulses. In one scene he attempts to reason with Squarciò, begging him to stop the dynamite fishing, arguing that it is environmentally damaging and dangerous. Squarciò's refusal of Gaspare's pleas leads to a compromising of Gaspare's position with his police superiors, who are annoyed that he has not arrested Squarciò. But Squarciò is uninterested in risking his earnings as a dynamite fisherman, which allow him to feed his family and buy exciting consumer goods, like a new radio. Thus Gaspare is forced out of his job and leaves the village. Like Domenico and Gaspare, the aging Santamaria is negatively influenced by Squarciò. Santamaria's attempt to copy Squarciò's dynamite fishing techniques also bucks the collective and family-based system of the fishing community. Santamaria is punished with the loss of an arm and the sale of his confiscated boat at auction.

The thematic climax of the film is when Squarciò—like the main characters in Vergano's *Outcry* and Pontecorvo's later films—overcomes his individual desires and gains a broader understanding of how his individualistic actions damage the fishermen's collective. For Squarciò the lesson arrives when he is mortally wounded, and he sends his sons home with his last words admitting that the fishermen of the cooperative are in the right. In the narrative the individualistic efforts of Squarciò and his eventual failure are necessary steps in the consolidation of collective consciousness among the next generation of fishermen, represented by Squarciò's sons Bore and Tonino.

The Wide Blue Road mixes neorealist elements (a common man story shot on location) with other elements thought to ensure box office success (name actors, color film). This kind of hybrid, combining commercial cinema with political engaged cinema, would later be defined as "pink neorealism." Pontecorvo later called the resulting film "mediocre."[10] Yet *The Wide Blue Road* displays interesting stylistic and ideological paradoxes, especially if considered in terms of Pontecorvo's subsequent features. In *The Wide Blue Road* Pontecorvo recounts a story about a community's struggle to act collectively instead of seeking individual gain. Squarciò's work as a dynamite fisherman represents the negative impact of individual initiative according to Pontecorvo's and Solinas's Marxist precepts. The individualistic main character is not a hero of the collective but rather the prime source of discord among his community of fishermen. *The Wide Blue Road* is basically a political parable: the defeat of a sympathetic antagonist affirms a progressive ideological position of collective action and condemns individualistic impulses. Pontecorvo and Solinas had already offered a similar story line in *Giovanna*, in which the protagonist, although ultimately victorious, jeopardizes familial tranquility by siding with the collective of the striking textile workers. In *The Wide Blue Road* the family unit also suffers from Squarciò's individualism, losing the family patriarch as well as Diana's first love, Domenico, to bomb blasts. As long as Pontecorvo and Solinas present their themes of beneficial collective action in microcosms like the Italian textile mill of *Giovanna* or the Mediterranean fishing village of *The Wide Blue Road*, their films are coherent examples of the political themes emanating from the neorealist tradition. However, for their next film, *Kapò*, Pontecorvo and Solinas would set their ideologically driven narrative in World War II and the Holocaust. The issues at hand in *Kapò* are not limited to economic competition and collective versus individual values, but include the specter of Nazi racist ideology.

NOTES

1. Irene Bignardi, *Memorie estorte a uno smemorato vita di Gillo Pontecorvo* (Milan: Feltrinelli, 1999), 86.

2. Lietta Tornabuoni, "Debutto d'autore," in *Gillo Pontecorvo Giovanna: Storia di un film e del suo restauro*, ed. Antonio Medici (Rome: Ediesse 2002), 13–14.

3. Tornabuoni, "Debutto d'autore."

4. See Tornabuoni, "Debutto d'autore."

5. Tornabuoni, "Debutto d'autore."

6. Tornabuoni, "Debutto d'autore."

7. Pam Cook, *The Cinema Book: A Complete Guide to Understanding the Movies*, 1st ed. (New York: Pantheon, 1985), 39.

8. See Marga Cottino-Jones, *A Student's Guide to Italian Cinema*, 2nd ed. (Dubuque, IA: Kendall Hunt, 1992).

9. In interviews Pontecorvo has reported that Montand apparently did not know how to swim, and the crew was forced to construct underwater planks so that he could mimic the actions of a swimmer.

10. Massimo Ghirelli, *Gillo Pontecorvo* (Firenze, Italy: La Nuova Italia, 1978), 13.

· 4 ·

Kapò (1960) and the Pitfalls of
Holocaust Re-creation

$\mathscr{A}$fter his debut directing *Le grande strada azzurra/The Wide Blue Road*, Pontecorvo and screenwriter Franco Solinas began to consider possible settings for a Holocaust drama. Pontecorvo had expressed interest in doing an adaptation of Dédé Lacaze's *The Tunnel*, the story of a deportee, a boxer, who survived by entertaining the SS with boxing matches and eventually escaped from the German camp at Mauthausen. Pontecorvo also read *The Moskat Family* by Isaac Bashevis Singer as well works by Joseph Roth and André Schwartz-Bart, including Schwartz-Bart's *The Last of the Just*.[1] But the work that struck Pontecorvo and Solinas as the most compelling account of the Holocaust was Primo Levi's *Se questo è un uomo/Survival in Auschwitz* (1947), in particular Levi's description of the manner in which Nazi SS guards and their trustees, called kapòs, ruthlessly denied prisoners' human dignity so that those who remained alive lived according to survival instincts stronger than any sense of national identity, personal dignity, class, or religion.

The story Pontecorvo and Solinas finally wrote for their first Academy Award–nominated film, *Kapò*, produced by Franco Cristaldi, depicts Edith, a fourteen-year-old Jewish girl from Paris, deported with her parents to a Nazi extermination camp. Unlike her parents, Edith is saved from the gas chambers by a kindly camp doctor who gives her the identity of a criminal prisoner named Nicole. Under her new identity Edith/Nicole is transferred to a work camp, where, through opportunism and cruelty, she rises to become a kapò. She becomes the mistress of an SS guard and then falls in love with a Russian prisoner who convinces her to make a heroic self-sacrificial attempt to arrange a mass escape for the other prisoners.

In the late 1950s the topic of the Nazi genocide of European Jewry and mass murder of other groups in work and extermination camps during World

War II had yet to become a frequent subject in feature films. The first Italian film on the Holocaust was *L'ebreo errante/The Wandering Jew* (1947), an adaptation of the novel by Eugène Sue (1804–1857) by a director, Goffredo Alessandrini, who had been active making war films during the Fascist era. Alessandrini's film, starring Vittorio Gasman, is an adaptation of the tale of the wandering Jew who scorned Jesus during the Passion and was punished with immortal suffering through the millennia.[2] Despite its intentions, the film has an unsettling undercurrent with its reference to the charge of deicide, which was an integral part of anti-Jewish propaganda. In the final sequences of Alessandrini's film, the wandering Jew, Mathieu Blumenthal, and his girl-friend, Ester, are imprisoned in a Nazi *lager*. The millennial curse is lifted when Mathieu offers to sacrifice himself for the survival of others, thus expiating his actions during the Passion. This plot sequence of a love story in a Nazi camp with the sacrifice of a Jew who expiates sins would be repeated by Pontecorvo in *Kapò*.

Kapò opens with the fourteen-year-old Parisian girl, Edith, at a piano lesson playing what seems to be a Bach fugue. The film immediately evidences the importance of music in Pontecorvo's work, as the sound track switches from the tones of the Bach-like fugue to a German military march and then to the title theme by Carlo Rustichelli, with a somber electric guitar solo on a background of violins. The sound track then returns to the theme of the fugue from Edith's piano lesson against the imagery of the train of deportees heading toward the camp. The musical theme that identifies Edith's original personality as an innocent Parisian girl resounds throughout the film. Pontecorvo has always insisted on the importance of music in his films. Beginning with his documentaries, Pontecorvo would compose musical themes at the piano and hire a music student to transcribe them. Pontecorvo has admitted to not possessing great ability in the technical aspects of film and has claimed he is always undecided about how to shoot a scene unless he has an idea of the music that will accompany it.[3]

In *Kapò*, Pontecorvo's main nod to his past as a neorealist documentarian is the use of grainy film stock to recreate the the look of neorealist films from the late 1940s. Pontecorvo attempted to give the film a documentary newsreel quality by using a type of film stock, Dupont 4, that is applicable to the technique of *controtipare*. According to Pontecorvo's description, in this technique the final print is made from a copy of the original negative, which is reexposed, causing a decrease in the quality of the film and resulting in a grainy newsreel hue. The same technique of *controtipare* was used in *La battaglia di Algeri/The Battle of Algiers* to much greater extent, since the technique was done twice.[4] Pontecorvo later admitted his regret regarding the relatively high visual quality of *Kapò* compared to the more newsreel-like effect he achieved in *The Battle of Algiers*. *Kapò* was also filmed by two camera crews: one led by Carlo di Palma and Marcello Gatti, then at the beginning of their careers, and another, Yugoslavian crew, which was part of the agreement for the Italo-Yugoslav coproduction. According to Pontecorvo, the Yugoslav crew had a tendency to film and light scenes in too professional a manner, contrary to Pontecorvo's attempt to give *Kapò* a documentary feel.[5]

Pontecorvo and screenwriter Solinas reportedly made efforts to interview Holocaust survivors and former camp SS guards so that the film would include elements of historical accuracy. In interviews Pontecorvo has often vaunted his ability as a filmmaker to arrive at a direct communication of the truth.[6] However, any attempt to recreate a historically accurate atmosphere would be difficult with an event as replete with narrative challenges as the Holocaust. Some scenes in *Kapò* are evocative of what has been later established as the historical processes by which the Nazis enacted the mass murder of European Jewry during World War II. For example, the portrayal of a crowd of Parisians passively watching as the Germans and French police truck off the Jews to be deported to the death camps gives an accurate idea of the low level of public resistance against the forced deportations in France. Within the camp the film vividly re-creates the violence of SS guards removing the deportees from the trains, the separation of mothers from children, and the selection of arrivals, with the fittest directed toward the camp and the weakest toward the gas chambers and crematoria. Pontecorvo offers these sequences with shot-countershot montages of anonymous close-ups that recall a formalist style. In these early scenes Pontecorvo's film affords the viewer an impression of the horror inflicted on the deportees. Yet the film's attempts at historical re-creation are overshadowed by characters who represent planks in the political ideology of the authors, which had already been expressed in the theme of collective versus individual in Pontecorvo's first feature, *The Wide Blue Road*.

In the Nazi death camp a political detainee, Sofia, brings the Parisian girl Edith to the attention of a sympathetic camp doctor. This camp doctor helps Edith after her improbable separation from a group of children awaiting their turn in the gas chambers. Given the historical reality of extermination camps, the attention lavished on Edith by the doctor is not entirely convincing. The steps taken by the doctor are conducted in an overtly personal fashion, whereas the actual course of experiences in the camps was brutally anonymous. The doctor lovingly shears Edith's hair, gives her an identifying tattoo, and gives her the black-triangled uniform of a dead criminal deportee named Nicole. The doctor saves Edith's life at the risk of his own in full awareness that Edith is Jewish. During Edith's assumption of the trappings of the dead Nicole, Pontecorvo allows Edith a privileged subjective camera view of naked deportees, including her parents and children, being marched toward the gas chambers. Ultimately Edith's view of her parents running naked toward their death and the scenes in which she listens to the doctor's advice about how to survive in the camp are narrative ploys meant to elicit audience response.

In Pontecorvo's defense, most Holocaust films are portrayals of exceptions. As a subject for a feature film, the Holocaust presents a sort of narrative black hole. The normal rules for a happy ending and pair bonding in classical comedy, or heroic or purgative death in classical tragedy, are difficult to apply to the brutal, industrialized mass murder conducted in the Nazi extermination camps.[7] Yet Pontecorvo's story of the Parisian girl Edith attempts to follow the rules of classical tragedy, whereby a protagonist redeems him- or herself in a heroic self-sacrifice. This approach denies the anonymous horror of the actual event and the lesson of authors like Primo Levi, whose accounts emphasize the manner in which the camps eliminated opportunities for higher emotions and reduced life to a brief, demeaning, horrific struggle for survival. It is no coincidence that the only film version of Primo Levi's writings depicts not his trials as a prisoner recounted in *Survival in Auschwitz* but Francesco Rosi's *La tregua/The Truce* (1997), an adaptation of Levi's account of his long journey home from Auschwitz to Turin after the war had ended.

With *Kapò*, Pontecorvo laid the path for future directors and producers to approach the Holocaust through stories with an individual perspective, even though, as Levi demonstrates so brilliantly in his accounts, such a perspective is exactly what the camps eliminated with ruthless efficiency. Pontecorvo's film is about an exception, a Jewish girl who assumes the identity of a political detainee. *Kapò* is among the first of what may be called "Holocaust exception narratives."[8] Later examples include Agnieszka Holland's *Europa, Europa* (1991), the story of Salomon Perel, the only Jew to join the Hitler Youth; Steven Spielberg's *Schindler's List* (1993), about the only German industrialist to save Jews; and Jack Gold's *Escape from Sobibor* (1987), about a rare documented revolt and escape from a death camp in Ukraine.[9] Pontecorvo's film about a Jewish girl who becomes a kapò is exactly the sort of narrative exception that has attracted film adaptation. However, the historical reality for a fourteen-year-old Jewish girl like the Parisian Edith in a Nazi death camp would not have made a very long film. An estimated 98 percent of deported children were killed immediately upon arrival.[10] Pontecorvo and Solinas's narrative invention—a young girl saved by camp medical staff who give her the identity of a deceased criminal detainee in order to help her survive—would have been extremely unlikely, if not an absolute impossibility.

There were few Italian films depicting Holocaust dramas into the late 1950s, with the exception of Alessandrini's *The Wandering Jew* and a sequence of

Jews praying before deportation in Roberto Rossellini's *Il Generale della Rovere/General della Rovere* (1959). After *Kapò* was released Carlo Lizzani, who had acted with Pontecorvo in *Il sole sorge ancora/Outcry*, directed *L'oro di Roma/The Gold of Rome* (1961), about the deportation of Roman Jews in 1943 and 1944. Later Italian films presented more visually pleasing portrayals of the deportations, such as Vittorio De Sica's bourgeois Holocaust drama, *Il giardino dei Finzi Continis/The Garden of the Finzi Continis* (1970), which, like Roberto Benigni's *La vita è bella/Life Is Beautiful* (1997), won an Oscar for best foreign film. In De Sica's film the spectator feels sympathy for the attractive and seminoble deportees Dominque Sanda. Lina Wertmuller's *Pasqualino Settebellezze/Seven Beauties* (1975), also nominated for a best foreign film Oscar, focuses on survival, with a depiction of barbaric executions by Nazis; in this film the characters are forced to consider their own culpability as Italians, Nazi Germany's allies in the war.[11] Both Benigni and De Sica avoid graphic depictions of the cruel reality of the deportations. Wertmuller, like Benigni, was criticized for profaning the Holocaust—in Wertmuller's case for scenes of an Italian prisoner's cynical copulation with the camp commandant and his later insistence on procreation as a means to ensure survival. Other Holocaust dramas include films that revert to an fable like narrative like Benigni's *Life Is Beautiful*, that refrain from attempts to depict the suffering inflicted in the camps, with the potentially dangerous assumption that the audience is well informed about the history of the Holocaust.[12]

Since Pontecorvo attempted a realistic recreation of the Holocaust, *Kapò* ultimately suffers from comparison with documentaries from the Allied armies, the hidden camera interviews of death camp personnel in Claude Lanzmann's documentary *Shoah* (1985), or Alain Resnais's use of postwar Allied army documentary footage of liberated camps in *Nuit et brouillard/Night and Fog* (1955) or *Memory of the Camps* (1985). Pontecorvo's later film *The Battle of Algiers* also has a more documentary and realistic feel than *Kapò*, which is due not only to the quality of the film stock but also to the film's characters and plot line, in which rhetoric about collectivity versus individuality is secondary to an attempt at historical re-creation.

Primo Levi's accounts benefit from his training as a chemist. As a scientist he was able to describe phenomena in objective terms in an echo of the Italian literary tradition of *verismo* (naturalism). The essential lesson of Primo Levi's account in *Survival in Auschwitz* is that the camps were an infernal microcosm, a world opposite in every way from any aspect of civil society. Since Pontecorvo's cinematic origins were in neorealist-style documentaries, he might have been expected to retain Levi's sense of objective portrayal, to let the facts speak for themselves. An event as horrific and inexcusable as the Holocaust has little need for narrative artifice. Pontecorvo's background in neorealist style documentaries did seem not prepare him for the breadth needed for historical recreation of an event with the narrative challenges of the Holocaust. The level of historical horror of the Holocaust was so immense that attempts at realistic re-creation can be of limited efficacy, especially when there is a recursion to narrative tropes (such as a love story) that are part of audience and producer expectations for the cinema.

Despite the fact that *Kapò* was made in black and white, it—like Pontecorvo's previous film, *The Wide Blue Road*—makes concessions to popular taste in the plot and story twists. As in some films of the early 1960s that depict the 1940s there is a certain sense of anachronism in the sets. When Edith passes in front of a Parisian street the store windows have clothes that seem to be from the late 1950s and not the early 1940s. There are flaws in actors' costumes, such as the 1960s hairdos of the protagonists. Such costume errors also hinder the historical representation in Lizzani's *L'oro di Roma/The Gold of Rome* (1961), another film that revolves around a love story.

Pontecorvo and Solinas also had difficulty with the casting of Susan Strasberg, the daughter of the then head of the New York Actors Studio, Lee Strasberg, in the starring role as Edith. Strasberg was cast at the suggestion of producer Franco Cristaldi after starring in the Pulitzer prize–winning stage production of *The Diary of Anne Frank* (1955) and appearing in Hollywood features including Joshua Logan's *Picnic* (1955). Pontecorvo had originally hoped to cast Claudia Cardinale, a budding sex symbol in the Italian cinema.[13] In fact the role of Edith requires an actress with sufficient sex appeal to be able to carry off scenes such as showing her breasts to the selection doctor to avoid showing the burns on her hands and to serve as a plausible concubine to the SS guards, thus gaining access to the kapò power structure and privileges. Besides having limited physical appeal, Strasberg is unconvincing as a sadistic and domineering kapò. Pontecorvo provided Strasberg with props such as a black cat named Faust and a riding crop in order to make her more believable in the role. Pontecorvo also had difficulty with Strasberg's method acting, a contrast in styles that would reoccur in Pontecorvo's legendary conflict with another method actor, Marlon Brando, on the set of *Queimada!/Burn!* (1969). Pontecorvo and his assistant director Giuliano Montaldo eventually stooped to the sort of neorealist directing methods that recall the staging tricks used to get animals to perform in wildlife documentaries. De Sica reportedly got Enzo Staiola, the child actor in *Ladri di biciclette/The Bicycle Thief*, to cry by planting cigarette butts in his pocket and accusing him of smoking; similarly, Pontecorvo provoked tears from Strasberg by having Montaldo slap her face and then berate her in front of the entire troupe for not being able to cry on cue, as would be expected of an actress of her reputation.[14]

Some of *Kapò*'s other casting inconsistencies also detract from the film's effectiveness. For example, in later interviews Pontecorvo has mentioned that his assistant directors canvassed nearby Yugoslav universities for female extras. These extras may have been attractive enough to be of romantic interest to Pontecorvo's assistants, but they are not entirely credible as starved slaves in a Nazi work camp.[15] Other actors cast in supporting roles also seem miscast, such as Lilli Perago, as the cynical political prisoner Sofia; Perago in fact appears too healthy to play a deportee sent to an extermination camp after not passing selection.

After the scenes in a Nazi extermination camp, Pontecorvo and Solinas wisely move Edith/Nicole to a work camp, where their narrative about individual versus collective values is more adaptable and the historical re-creation more believable. In the opening scenes at the work camp Pontecorvo effectively portrays the horror of selection, in which prisoners attempt to make themselves appear healthier by putting blood on their checks to affect a rosy complexion or mud in their hair to hide the gray. The work details are presented with a similar sense of cruelty and abjection. However once the setting moves to the work camp Pontecorvo and Solinas fill the script with plot machinations and characters constructed to impart moral lessons that recall the plots of *Giovanna* and *The Wide Blue Road. Kapò* is filled with rhetorical flourishes about moral responsibility and identity, characterizations that are superfluous in an environment whose very makeup is enough to condemn them.

The main narrative inconsistency in *Kapò* is the inclusion of a love story in the film. Some of Solinas's early screenplays, besides *Giovanna* and *The Wide Blue Road*, feature melodramatic love stories. *Persiane chiuse/Behind Closed Shutters* (1950), directed by Luigi Comencini, is the story of a woman who falls into prostitution. *Bella non piangere* (1954), directed by Davide Carbonari, is about a World War I hero who overcomes the loss of a leg in a train accident. Solinas's script for the Gina Lollobrigida vehicle and box office hit *La donna più bella del mondo/ The Most Beautiful Woman in the World* (1955) ends with a happy love story. *I fidanzati della morte* (1957), directed by Romolo Marcellini, is about motorcycle enthusiasts in love. *The Savage Innocents* (1959), directed by Nicolas Ray, is a noble savage story in which an Eskimo, played by Anthony Quinn, encounters difficulties with the civilized world. Some of the elements from Solinas's previous scripts creep into *Kapò*, particularly in the love story involving Nicole and a Russian prisoner of war, Sasha, played by future director Laurent Terzieff. Pontecorvo later reported heated disagreements with Solinas regarding the inclusion of a love story in *Kapò*. The break in their collaboration was resolved only when the producer of the film threatened remove his support.[16] With the eventual inclusion of Solinas's improbable love story in the setting of a Nazi camp, *Kapò* becomes a film that recalls the pink neorealism of *The Wide Blue Road*, due to the concessions made within the film's narrative in anticipation of audience reaction.

The love story in *Kapò* could be read in terms of the screenwriters' efforts to offer characters as representatives of the moral lesson of collective versus individual values. In Pontecorvo and Solinas's previous films, like *The Wide Blue Road*, characters who seek personal economic gain either die, like Squarciò and Domenico, or are maimed, like the aging Santamaria. As in *The Wide Blue Road*, the script of *Kapò* separates characters who have a sense of collective responsibility from those who lack this moral awareness. Like the individualistic fisherman Squarciò in *The Wide Blue Road*, the prisoners who rise to become kapòs are betrayers of the collective group, in this case of prisoners. *Kapò* even has references to the kapòs' interest in fashion magazines and smart Nazi uniforms. The film could be read as a melodrama in which Edith's attempts to remain alive are not only about survival but also about elevating her class status within the world of the camp. The essence of the kapò mindset is in the brief exchanges between Nicole and the head kapò, Alice, who is eager to share news of an opportunity for Nicole to be promoted to the position of kapò. For even in a Nazi *lager* there is a social ladder to climb. Once Edith completes the transformation into Nicole the kapò, she accepts the power that comes with her new role. As a newly appointed kapò Nicole quickly assumes the garb and attitudes of a kapò, with a smart uniform, riding crop, and a black cat named Faust; and she beats Georgette, a criminal prisoner who dares to question her authority.

As *Kapò* follows the transformation of the innocent Parisian piano student Edith into a jaded and sadistic Nazi camp trustee, Pontecorvo and Solinas offer a supporting cast of characters whose philosophies must be read as attempts by the screenwriters to frame Edith's decision in terms of a contrast between individualistic versus collective values. There is Katia, the Polish girl interested in retaining contact with her Polish family and national identity. Teresa is an educated political detainee who was active in the resistance and serves as camp translator. Sofia is another political prisoner, but illness weakens her moral resolve, so that she becomes as cynical as any of the criminal prisoners. Carole, the head of the political prisoners, is idealistic and organizes her comrades in sabotages of camp machinery and escape attempts. Anna is an unassuming Russian woman who is ecstatic when Russian soldiers arrive. Georgette, the spokesperson of the criminal prisoners, is cynical and mean-spirited. Alice is a kapò who maintains a materialistic outlook throughout the film and facilitates Nicole's promotion. With this cast of characters Pontecorvo and Solinas make points about human nature, identity, and moral positioning in ideological terms that recall the collective-versus-individualistic story line from *The Wide Blue Road*. The division between the fishermen in favor of a collective and the dynamite fisherman Squarciò from *The Wide Blue Road* becomes the division between political and criminal detainees in *Kapò*. The political detainees are more idealistic, generous, and conscious of higher motivations in life. Those condemned for more traditional crimes are marked with the black triangle of criminal prisoners. They are cynical and shallow, and they provide the bulk of the kapòs. The political prisoners insist on their superior moral position to the point that there is a schism within the barracks between the political and criminal detainees. These tensions play out in Edith/Nicole's moral dilemma in choosing between collaboration, which might mean survival, or retention of her previous identity as a well-bred Parisian Jewish girl, which would more likely lead to death.

Edith's successful struggle to rise in the camp begins when she meets Teresa, the political prisoner and camp translator, played by Emmanuelle Riva, fresh from her role in Alain Resnais's *Hiroshima Mon Amour* (1959). Central to Teresa's sense of identity is her status as a political prisoner. The nucleus of political prisoners plot escape, sabotage, and resistance, themes dear to Pontecorvo from his days in the anti-Nazi/Fascist resistance in World War II. Teresa, as the archetypal idealistic political prisoner, gives the newly arrived Edith a speech about the importance of washing oneself in order to maintain a semblance of human dignity. Yet Teresa also realizes that Edith is Jewish and masquerading as the criminal prisoner Nicole. By lying to Teresa and denying her Jewish identity, Edith/Nicole shows that she has begun to understand that codes of civilized behavior no longer apply in the camp, a first step in her rise to the position of kapò. Edith/Nicole then steals food, an act that historically provoked extreme sanctions from within the ranks of prisoners. As Nicole rises and gains strength through such acts, the idealistic Teresa declines. She ultimately breaks down when forced to translate the camp commander's warnings to camp population regarding Carole, the head political prisoner, who awaits the gallows for sabotaging camp equipment. The commander's explanation of the camp as operating based on a rational economic relationship between the prisoners, who supply labor, and the Nazi Reich, which supplies food, is too much for Teresa. She is tearfully unable to translate the commandant's speech and is punished with three months' half rations and fifteen days in solitary confinement, a sentence that dooms her to slow starvation. When Teresa returns to the barracks and steals a fellow prisoner's ration of bread, repeating Nicole's earlier theft, she is met with the cynical scorn of Nicole, who cruelly reminds her of her previous advice about retaining human dignity. In response Teresa commits suicide by running into the electric fence surrounding the camp.

Pontecorvo's close-up on the face of the dead Teresa on the electric fence as the other prisoners file by was heavily criticized by French filmmaker and critic Jacques Rivette as being an "abject" denial of the humanity of the character. Rivette's main interest in the review is not Pontecorvo's film as much as the difficulty and inappropriateness of attempting to recreate reality using the artifice of the fictional film, which will inevitably fall short of the actual camp liberation documentary footage of works like Resnais's *Nuit et brouillard/ Night and Fog*.[17] Pontecorvo's choreography of Teresa's suicide includes a sustained shot of the corpse of the dead woman that emphasizes a lack of reaction from the other inmates, who file by her lifeless body. Due to Pontecorvo's composition of the scene, Teresa's suicide seems more like a defeat than an act affirming individualism. The shot that offends Rivette—the pan and zoom in on the body of the dead Teresa as the other prisoners mutely file by—does not exalt her suicide as an expression of a stubborn individuality in the face of defeat. Rivette's condemnation of the scene may actually derive from the French literary and filmic tradition of heroic and romantic suicide.[18] An oft repeated narrative pattern in French cinema emphasizes the sense of individual panache in suicide, from that of Jean Gabin in Duvivier's *Pépé le Moko* (1936) to that of Gerard Depardieu in *Vatel* (2000). Pontecorvo responded to Rivette's comments by explaining that this famous tracking shot in *Kapò* is actually a rapid zoom shot intended to demonstrate how the camps made death a common occurrence.[19] Thus the lack of reaction from the passing prisoners is an indication of the loss of humanity within the camp.

In terms of the narrative structure of the film Teresa's death is a turning point for Nicole, who begins to waver in her conviction that she should continue as a kapò. This narrative ploy of using an execution scene as a moment in which a character reaches a moral crossroads recalls Pontecorvo's experience on Vergano's *Outcry*, in which Pontecorvo, as the resistance fighter Pietro, and Carlo Lizzani, as a Catholic priest, are executed by a Nazi firing squad. In *Kapò* the execution of Carole, the head political prisoner, is a point of no return for Teresa, as similar deaths would be points of no return for later Pontecorvo characters, like Ali Le Pointe in *The Battle of Algiers* when he witnesses an Algerian activist being killed on the guillotine. In each film the witnessing of an execution becomes a moment of political realization for the protagonists.

Besides creating a minor critical stir between Rivette and Pontecorvo, the exchanges between Teresa and Edith/Nicole actually reveal an unsettling, but central, aspect of the narrative. Since the film opens with scenes in a Nazi extermination camp, it is curious that the film does not emphasize the racism in Nazi ideology. In fact the thematic conflict in the film is between criminal and political detainees rather than between Nazis and anti-Nazis. The only rationale presented in the film for the Nazi camp system is the inane explanation given by the camp commandant, haltingly translated by Teresa, before the hanging of Carole, the head of the political prisoners, who is executed for sabotaging camp equipment. The Nazi commandant defines camp life as a rational exchange between the Reich, which supplies food, and the prisoners, who supply labor. But the film has limited references to the racial prejudice that was at the center of Nazi ideology. Teresa is the only character in the camp who identifies Edith as a Jew. When Nicole admits that she is Jewish to her love interest, the Russian prisoner Sasha, he receives the news with numb indifference and provides her with improbable assurances that after liberation his Russian family will welcome her despite her paradoxical past as a Jewish kapò. Besides the uniforms, the language of the camp guards, military marches from the camp loudspeaker, and occasional shots of a period photo of Hitler in the SS quarters, there is little emphasis on elements that make the camp a place for the implementation of Nazi racist ideology. With some costume and set changes the work camp in *Kapò* could be a prison camp in any totalitarian system.

After the scenes of the arrest of Edith's family in Paris and the depictions of the extermination camp, Edith is the only surviving Jew in the film. Pontecorvo's film presents a work camp in which the division between political and criminal prisoners indicates their stance on issues of collective responsibility, a theme that recalls Pontecorvo and Solinas's fishing village drama *The Wide Blue Road*. But *Kapò* also has an ethnic context, since differences between prisoners are presented in terms of national origin. There are different nationalities among the prisoners of war, including a Royal Air Force pilot who works with his Russian comrades as an indication of the collective unity of Allied forces. The film features prisoners representing various nationalities of the European continent who suffer not only the brutal attempt at world conquest by the Nazi regime, but also the opportunistic and venal rise to the dominant position of kapò by the only Jewish character in the film, Edith/Nicole. Edith's ability to rise to kapò through unsavory means could be read as a repetition of the commonplaces about Jewish venality and opportunism central to the history of anti-Semitism as well as a Nazi rationale for the Final Solution. Edith opens the film as an innocent girl, but eventually she exhibits negative characteristics to the point that the director arrays her in the trappings of a B movie villain, with a riding crop and black cat named Faust to accompany her statements rationalizing a hedonistic outlook on life. Edith/Nicole finally achieves personal redemption by sacrificing herself for the collective escape of the other prisoners, but like all the Jews in the film, she is eventually killed by the SS. The Jews in the opening extermination camp sequences are murdered with little explanation of the ideological context of Nazism, as if the context of the Holocaust is information that the screenwriters assume is part of the collective knowledge of the spectators.[20]

The narrative of *Kapò*, with Edith's commission of affronts, self-sacrifice, and final redemption, recalls the first Italian Holocaust film, Alessandrini's

L'ebreo errante/The Wandering Jew (1947). In Alessandrini's film the Jewish protagonist, Mathieu Blumenthal, makes a millennial journey through history after being cursed with immortality for having scorned Jesus during the Passion. In *The Wandering Jew* internment in a Nazi camp becomes an opportunity for Mathieu to expiate his sin of the age-old plank of anti-Jewish propaganda of deicide. The curse is lifted when Mathieu shows himself willing to sacrifice himself for his fellow prisoners. In *Kapò* Pontecorvo and Solinas repeat the narrative of *The Wandering Jew*, in which the Jewish character achieves redemption through self-sacrifice after behaving in a manner that recalls anti-Semitic propaganda. The perhaps unintentional but troubling undertone of both films is that in these films European Jews, even if represented by a seemingly innocent figure like Edith, display anticollective character traits. Pontecorvo and Solinas had already made a film, *The Wide Blue Road*, in which the antagonist, the individualistic dynamite fisherman Squarciò, works against the collective for his own benefit. Squarciò's final demise benefits the community of fishermen, as his model of individual initiative is proven to be a false path for his fishing community. Like Squarciò, Nicole is self-serving and uninterested in the collective well-being of her fellow prisoners. The trouble with transferring this theme from the strictly economic and interfamilial story line of Squarciò's fishing village in *The Wide Blue Road* to a story featuring a Jew deported to a Nazi camp during the immense suffering of World War II is that, given the historical continuity of anti-Semitism in Europe, the theme is simply too limited to contain the larger racist context of the Holocaust.

Pontecorvo's perhaps unwitting repetition of the story line from *The Wandering Jew* in *Kapò* raises questions about his own commitment to or sense of Jewish identity. Pontecorvo has admitted that, like some Italian Jews, the members of his family were assimilated and nonpracticing, and they never considered their identity until the progressive attacks on their civil rights that began with the Italian Fascist regime's *leggi raziali* (racial statutes), passed in September of 1938.[21] These laws prevented Jews from holding public office, attending public school, intermarriage, and ownership of more than a limited amount of real estate, and they caused a diaspora of the Pontecorvo family. The identification of a potential, if involuntary, unsettling undertone in *Kapò* also raises questions about the subsequent rise of anti-Jewish attitudes among politically progressive factions in Europe, which has increasingly been identified in the context of traditional, European anti-Semitism.[22]

Besides emphasizing the ideological and moral division between political and criminal prisoners, the script pays close attention to national origin. Despite Pontecorvo's claim that the film was influenced by Primo Levi's *Survival in Auschwitz*, the film does not adequately communicate Levi's point that the camps were run in such a way as to remove all sense of human identification from the prisoners. Instead Pontecorvo and Solinas insist on the importance of national identification throughout the film. When the prisoners first march toward the camp, a Polish prisoner, Katia, receives bread from a Polish train worker in a gesture of national solidarity. The Russian prisoner, Anna, comforts Katia and says that the Russian Red Army will arrive to save her, another reference to national pride and identity. When the male Russian prisoners arrive they sing a nationalistic fight song, "Holy War," another expression of pride, before Anna, the Russian prisoner, embraces the POWs as her children.

The film's emphasis on national identity breaks down not in the characterization of the prisoners but in the figure of Karl, the taciturn, one-armed German SS guard who has a relationship with Nicole. When Nicole asks Karl what is important to him, he gives an answer expected of German soldiers of his generation—that his country is everything. But the maimed Karl is an unconvincing representative of the nationalistic arrogance that fired Nazi Germany. He does not spout any of the expected Nazi theories about social Darwinism, nor does he offer any mention of racial prejudice. The essence of the Nazi movement—with its racist impetus so central to the SS, the political cadre of the German army charged with running Nazi camps—is not adequately mentioned in the film. Karl's rationale for the cruelties he inflicts is reduced to a stale mantra of national sentiment.

Despite the attempt to use the setting of a Nazi work *lager* to frame the authors' ideas about collective values versus individual values, the essence of the narrative relies not on ideological but on sexual elements. The transformation that takes Edith from her first identity as an innocent Parisian schoolgirl to the cynical kapò Nicole is above all a sexual process. The trailer used to advertise the film presented Susan Strasberg's nude back as Edith first dons the uniform of the deceased criminal deportee, Nicole. The sexual transformation of Edith to Nicole continues when she cleverly displays her breasts to the examining Nazi doctor as a ruse to avoid having to reveal the wounds on her hands, which would have marked her for transfer back to an extermination camp. Edith then accepts an invitation from the SS guards to trade her virginity for food, a move that allows her to meet her benefactor, Karl, the taciturn, one-armed German SS guard.

The film has been criticized for the love story between Nicole and Sasha the Russian prisoner, but perhaps the more important amorous relationship in the film is actually between Karl, the SS guard, and Nicole. In the scene in which Nicole is brought before the SS to provide sexual diversion, she cowers meekly. After her sexual submission she asks for food, but the SS derisively tell her to return tomorrow. The next sequence is a flash forward: Edith's hair has grown and she consorts with Karl on equal terms, comfortable in the guards' quarters in her identity as Nicole during her second Christmas at the camp. The small talk between Nicole and Karl about his memories of the Nazi's conquering parade in Paris as they play cards supposedly shows the inanity of life without a sense of moral conviction. When Nicole asks Karl what he will do if Germany loses the war, he cannot even accept the premise. With these scenes Pontecorvo approaches what would be one of his strengths as a director and screenwriter—the ability to depict the reasoning behind all sides in a conflict. This ability is also evident in the portrayal of Ben M'hidi and Mathieu in *The Battle of Algiers* and Walker and Josè Dolores in *Burn!* But in *Kapò* the opposing ideologies, the duality in life philosophies that is emphasized in the film is between political and criminal deportees rather than between Nazis and anti-Nazis. The film's Nazis are unconvincing proponents of the presumptuous attitudes that led Germany to self-destruction in two world wars. Karl's only expression of self-consciousness is a dull nationalism that contrasts the hedonism of the solider who deflowers Edith. In a later conversation Karl explains to Nicole that he is bored by the camp and has requested transfer back to the front, even though he only has one arm. When Karl repeats Nicole's question about what is important in life, Nicole responds that she is happy, since all of her physical needs are met. Thus as a kapò Nicole copies the dull hedonism of Karl's SS comrades. Before the last escape sequences of the film, Nicole and Karl have a brief exchange in which they agree that being alive is not really necessary. Their outlook on life degrades from a pathetic hedonism to a stale nihilism.

Given the duration and repetition of scenes involving Karl and Nicole, it is curious that Pontecorvo and Solinas thought it necessary to include another love story, between Nicole and a Russian prisoner of war, Sasha. The Russian prisoner of war appears in the film as a political icon, a sort of heroic Soviet solider. His brief contact with Nicole is enough to convince her not only to help the other prisoners but to sacrifice herself to do so. The sequences of the love story between Sasha and Nicole are among the most unconvincing of the film. Their courtship is consumed after a night of terror for Sasha provoked by Nicole, in which he must stand attention next to the electric fence for the entire night. If he moves backward he will be shot, if he moves forward he will be electrocuted by the fence. The next morning Edith offers Sasha bread and margarine, which he proudly refuses in a complete break with the actual life in the camps. When Sasha hears distant artillery and tells Nicole that the war will end, the pair meet in a barn or between the barracks and have a romantic interlude on the mud.

The intent of the screenwriters seems to have been to make Sasha into a character who could repeat the moral discourses offered by Teresa, the political prisoner who identified Edith as Jew and appealed to her conscience.

In the plot the love story between Nicole and Sasha should function as a moral turning point for Nicole, who, due to remorse following the suicide of Teresa and her affection for Sasha, is suddenly willing to sacrifice herself for the escape of the prisoners she had previously treated with such cruelty. In the final sequences of the film, Nicole, like Teresa, makes a self-sacrificial run to turn off the power to the electric fence, facilitating the mass escape attempt of the other prisoners. After Nicole turns off the power, Karl mortally wounds her with a burst of machine gun fire. Nicole then dies in Karl's arms and tells him, "They tricked us Karl, both of us," a statement of unexpected solidarity between a Jewish deportee and her SS murderer. Nicole then asks Karl to take off her kapò uniform so she may chant a Jewish death prayer and die in his arms, reacquiring her Jewish identity as Edith. Perhaps the scene is an attempt by Pontecorvo and Solinas to contextualize the nationalistic impulse that led Germany to rationalize an attempt at world conquest and genocide and Nicole's impulse to survive in the camp by becoming a kapò. The ending is consistent if it is interpreted as a sequel to the suicide of Teresa, the deportee who had encouraged Nicole to maintain her dignity, and who killed herself on the electric fence after being scorned by Nicole. Pontecorvo has revealed that during the screenwriting process he actually suggested that Nicole survive the escape attempt. The other deportees would celebrate their freedom, but Edith/Nicole would remain in a state of solitude and despair over her collaboration with the side that murdered her parents and forced her to reject her identity as Edith, an innocent girl from a good family. Pontecorvo even proposed that the film end without any settling of scores against Edith/Nicole, but only with a sense of her tremendous and tragic solitude.[23] But this ending was discarded, and the actual ending was improvised as dictated by the atmosphere on the set.[24] Instead of Edith/Nicole, the figure featured in the final shots of the film is the Russian prisoner Sasha, who, after improbably surviving the escape attempt, stands weeping among the bodies of dead prisoners. These final shots of Sasha can be interpreted only as making him a political symbol. Sasha, the good Russian solider, represents the coming of a new era in European history in which the collective ideals of a Marxist state rule after the defeat of the Nazis.

Kapò remains an important attempt by commercial cinema to depict the Holocaust. However the film is conditioned by a theatrical presentation and a narrative that indicate the difficulties in depicting the Nazi's attempt at the genocide of European Jewry and mass murder during World War II. The rise of the deportee Edith to the status of kapò and her subsequent decision to sacrifice herself so her fellow inmates may escape puts the film into the category of the Holocaust exception film, in which the thematic emphasis is on the story of an individual whose experience is unique within the industrialized mass murder orchestrated by the Nazi regime. However, the shift from a setting in an extermination camp, where ethnic identity was a central factor in the mass murders of the Nazis, to a work camp, where in Pontecorvo's recreation the differences between political and criminal deportees had more weight, sidesteps the specter of anti-Semitism and racism so important in Nazi ideology and so imbedded in European history. Since the Jewish character, Edith, rises in the work camp to the status of kapò through actions that repeat propaganda historically leveled against European Jewry, the film has unsettling narrative elements in common with the Italy's first Holocaust drama, Alessandrini's film *The Wandering Jew.*

NOTES

1. Irene Bignardi, *Memorie estorte a uno smemorato vita di Gillo Pontecorvo* (Milan: Feltrinelli, 1999), 106.
2. Carlo Celli, *The Divine Comic: The Cinema of Roberto Benigni* (Lanham, MD: Scarecrow, 2001).
3. Gillo Pontecorvo, "Interview," *Kapò,* DVD (Rome: Cristaldi Film, 2004).
4. Pontecorvo, "Interview."
5. Pontecorvo, "Interview."
6. See Oliver Curtis, *Pontecorvo: The Dictatorship of Truth,* in *The Battle of Algiers,* DVD (Irvington, NY: Rialto Pictures, 2004).
7. Carlo Celli, "Interview with Marcello Pezzetti," *Critical Inquiry* 27 (Autumn 2000): 149–57.
8. Celli, "Interview," 149–57.
9. Celli, *Divine Comic.*
10. Celli, "Interview," 149–57.
11. Celli, *Divine.*
12. Celli, *Divine.*
13. Pontecorvo, "Interview."
14. Pontecorvo, "Interview."
15. Pontecorvo, "Interview."
16. Pontecorvo, "Interview."
17. See J. Rivette, "De l'abjection," *Les cahiers du cinema* 20, no. 120 (1961): 54–55.
18. See Victor Brombert, *The Intellectual Hero: Studies in the French Novel, 1880–1955* (Chicago: University of Chicago Press, 1960).
19. Pontecorvo, "Interview."
20. The danger of assuming an awareness of the Holocaust is also one of the backdrops for the criticism of Roberto Benigni's film *La vita è bella/Life Is Beautiful* (1997). See Carlo Celli, "The Representation of Evil in Roberto Benigni's *La vita è bella/Life Is Beautiful," Journal of Popular Film and Television* 28, no. 2 (Summer 2000): 74–79.

21. Bignardi, *Memorie*, 13.

22. See Fiamma Nirentein, *Gli antisemiti progressisti la forma nuova di un odio antico* (Milan: Rizzoli, 2004).

23. Pontecorvo, "Interview."

24. Bignardi, *Memorie*, 109.

The Two Endings of
La battaglia di Algeri/
The Battle of Algiers (1966)

Gillo Pontecorvo directing a crowd scene in The Battle of Algiers.
Courtesy of Springer/Photofest

After *Kapò*, Pontecorvo reportedly received offers from producers interested in hiring a director recently nominated for an Academy Award. However, Pontecorvo rejected many worthy films; a pattern he later ascribed to a character flaw of not being able to commit to a project that did not convince him absolutely.[1] In the years following the release of *Kapò* Pontecorvo did participate in Fausta Leoni's *Karma storia autentcia di una reincarnazione/Karma: The Story of an Authentic Reincarnation*, a documentary about the eternal questions of life that was proposed to and rejected by the Italian state television network, RAI.

As part of Pontecorvo's library of unfinished projects, in the early 1960s Pontecorvo and Solinas wrote a treatment for a film to be called *Para*, about a young French parachute soldier working for the magazine *Paris Match* who wants to get closer to the action of the independence movement in Algeria. This Pontecorvo-Solinas treatment is apparently imbedded with an admiration for the cool, macho professionalism of the French paratroopers.[2] Pontecorvo reportedly contacted Paul Newman and Warren Beatty about starring in the film, but the film was never made, in part because producers at the time were of wary of the Organisation de l'Armée Secrète (OAS), a terrorist group active in maintaining French rule in Algeria through intimidation and terrorism. Pontecorvo had traveled to Algeria in order to do research for *Para* in 1962, posing as a journalist. There, he made contacts with the Algerian National Liberation Front (FLN)—the organization that led the fight for independence from France. Pontecorvo reportedly stayed until the Evian accords of March 18, 1962, which granted Algeria sovereignty and ended the Franco-Algerian conflict.[3]

After Algeria achieved independence, Algerian producers, on the orders of Jacef Saadi, one of the historic heads of the Algerian resistance, came to Europe with a script by Salah Baazi. They were searching for a director to make a film about the Algerian national story of liberation from France. Due to the recent war for independence, the Algerians were wary of contracting a French director for their project. The Italian film industry of the early 1960s had developed a genre of film that would come to be known as the *film politico* (political film) that offered direct representation of political and social problems. The Italian political film genre is often considered to be the heir of the neorealist school of the 1940s. When the Algerians came to Italy they were well aware of the Italian film industry's ability to handle political themes. In the early 1960s the Italian film industry was the second producer of films worldwide, taking advantage of the retrenchment of the Hollywood industry due mainly to the competition from television, a situation that would not affect the Italian film industry until the 1970s.

For their film the Algerians had in mind directors including Francesco Rosi and Luchino Visconti. But these directors already had commitments and were thus unavailable to work on a film about Algeria.[4] When the Algerians approached Pontecorvo, he reportedly felt that the Baazi script was too propagandistic and pro-Algerian. Conversely, the Algerians felt that the Pontecorvo/Solinas treatment of the French paratrooper *Para* had an excessively European point of view. When Pontecorvo proposed to write a new script about the formation of the Algerian nation with the initial title *You Will Be*

Brahim Haggiag (Ali La Pointe) far right and Yacef Saadi (as Djafar—himself)
second from the left in The Battle of Algiers. *Courtesy of Photofest*

Born with Pain, the Algerians agreed. Pontecorvo signed with Casbah Films, a production company controlled by the Algerian government. However, the Algerians were able to cover less than half the production costs, and Pontecorvo was forced to seek funding elsewhere—a difficult task, since producers were reticent to invest in what they determined was an Arab story with a documentary tone unlikely to arouse much commercial interest. Pontecorvo was eventually able to make the film with the help of producer Antonio Musu and loans granted after Italian theatrical associations guaranteed the film enough distribution to satisfy banking requirements.[5]

This financial independence allowed Pontecorvo to give free rein to a cinematic vision of the story of Algerian independence using many of the stylistic elements of Italian neorealism. The neorealist style of Italian films of the late 1940s was an aesthetic approach that was conditioned by the dearth of resources such as studios and electricity in immediate postwar Italy. Pontecorvo and his crew went to extreme lengths to re-create this neorealist style in *La battaglia di Algeri/The Battle of Algiers*. The film was shot in black and white with a somber tonality. At times the sets were reportedly covered so that the bright light of Algiers would not reflect the sun. In fact in the film the sunny Mediterranean climate of Algiers appears as an almost Baltic gray.[6] Because of Pontecorvo's close relationship with the Algerian government, his production was allowed access to locations in the city of Algiers and its Casbah. Pontecorvo doubled the *controtipare* technique of reexposing film stock used for *Kapò* to give *The Battle of Algiers* a newsreel tone. In fact, the care taken by Pontecorvo's crew to recreate the heroic and convincing documentary style of Italian neorealism with casting, on-location shooting, and the use of film stock to create a newsreel tone was more complete than in *Kapò*. *The Battle of Algiers* has the stark style and reduced narrative embellishments that recall Pontecorvo's first film, *Giovanna*. The result is a film that offers a convincing recreation of a neorealist style and that had to be advertised as not containing any documentary footage. Pontecorvo cast the illiterate nonprofessional actor Brahim Haggiag as the protagonist, Ali La Pointe. The film also features Jacef Saadi, a historical leader of FLN cells in the city of Algiers. Saadi plays Kader, basically himself, in the film. The setting of the film in a period of a clandestine, urban armed struggle also allowed Pontecorvo to evoke his own experiences and memories of the Italian resistance of World War II. Therefore *The Battle of Algiers* effectively combines Pontecorvo's memories with the recollections of Saadi, giving the film an undeniable sense of authenticity.

Pontecorvo's film before *The Battle of Algiers*, *Kapò*, has narrative ploys, such as the improbable love story between a Jewish kapò and a Russian prisoner of war in a Nazi work *lager*, that actually detract from the film's depiction of the historical period of Nazi slave camps and attempt at genocide of European Jewry in the Holocaust. With *The Battle of Algiers*, Pontecorvo made a conscious attempt to reduce traditional narrative elements. A love story between two of the FLN activists is reduced to a sequence of a marriage ceremony instead of becoming a central part of the plot, as in *Kapò* or Pontecorvo's last film, *Ogro*, which features two Basque terrorists in love.

The voice-over narration in *The Battle of Algiers* provides specific references to dates in the history of the Algerian rebellion in a style that recalls Pontecorvo's early documentaries. The near absence of audience-anticipated narrative ploys, like love stories, and the use of documentary-style voice-overs results in a temptation to accept the historical veracity of the film, and in fact the influence of the film has been lasting. A disclaimer had to be placed on the film's trailer announcing that the film had no documentary footage because of the effectiveness of Pontecorvo's re-creation of a documentary style.

Even with the attention given to elements that enhance the realistic tone of the film, it is a challenge to give a spectator a complete or even summary idea of the history of a country as complex as Algeria or an event as travailed as the Franco-Algerian war in the confines of a feature-length, commercial film. As screenwriters, Pontecorvo and Solinas were forced to make difficult choices. The city of Algiers has an ancient history, with periods of domination by Carthage, Rome, and the Muslim caliphate of the Fatimid dynasty and the Turkish Ottoman Empire beginning in the sixteenth century. The city was a center of Barbary pirate activity before French invasions began in the 1830s against resistance mainly in the interior regions. By 1848 Algeria had been declared a French territory, with an influx of permanent colonial settlements. There was no sustained Algerian independence movement until after World War II, when Algerians who recalled French general de Gaulle's statements about national self-determination during World War II were repressed by French forces. In 1954 the FLN rebellion against French rule began; in the conflict both sides targeted civilians. Random shootings of French civilians and policemen caused the reaction of *pied noir* (black foot) French colonialists, who in 1955 set a bomb in the Casbah of Algiers, killing many. This in turn led to FLN retaliation in 1956 with three bombings in the French quarter. The actual Battle of Algiers referred to in the title of the film began when French paratroopers cleared the city of FLN militants including leader Ben M'hidi, who was arrested and subsequently died mysteriously in prison the same year. The film opens with a depiction of events in August 1957, when FLN guerilla Ali Le Pointe is blown up in the Casbah with twelve-year-old Omar and Hassiba Ben Bouli by French forces after refusing to surrender.

By focusing on the Battle of Algiers period, the film leaves out important events in the history of Algerian independence. The film does not mention 1958 demonstrations in France against French president de Gaulle's concessions to the Algerian independence movement. It ignores the larger historical context of the defeat of French colonialism in Vietnam in 1954 and the failure of the Anglo-French invasion of the Suez Canal in 1956. The film does not mention the mutiny of French troops after de Gaulle moved toward a policy of allowing independence and self-determination for Algeria. Nor is there any specific treatment of the rise of the OAS, which opposed Algerian independence and conducted a terrorist campaign that included attempts on the life of de Gaulle. There is only a brief allusion to the manner in which colonists conducted the infamous *ratonnades* (lynching and death squads) with the collusion of the authorities. There is little mention of events in the Algerian hinterland, where the French army actually lost control of the territory, in part because the hundreds of thousands of French *pied noirs* were concentrated in urban zones, thus facilitating French control of those areas.

Instead of providing a larger historical overview, *The Battle of Algiers* concentrates on the period from 1954 to 1957 known as the "Battle of Algiers," in which French paratroopers quashed the FLN rebellion in the city of

Algiers. The film concludes with an epilogue depicting popular uprisings in the city of Algiers in 1960, in which the commander of the French forces is not Mathieu but an anonymous figure speaking into a megaphone, and a brief voice-over referring to the 1962 accord signed by the French government for a cease-fire and eventual independence. In effect Pontecorvo's film has two endings. In one ending French paratroopers successfully destroy the insurgency in the city of Algiers. In the last scenes portraying the French commander Mathieu, he has been able to eliminate the last FLN cell in the city. Therefore the film portrays his efforts in a victorious light. But by adding a coda depicting the popular revolts before eventual independence, the film also portrays the FLN as having been effective in the creation of national consciousness among the Algerian populace.

As with *Kapò*, *The Battle of Algiers* is a staged reproduction of a historical period dependent on the director's narrative choices and strategies. The period between 1954 and 1957 known as the "Battle of Algiers," when French paratroopers and counterterrorist units successfully, although temporarily, subdued an insurgency in the capital city Algiers, obviously reminded Pontecorvo of his experiences in the anti-Nazi resistance during World War II. The setting of *The Battle of Algiers* in the period of 1954 to 1957 anoints the FLN with the status of victim, which partly attenuates the moral reprehensibility of the FLN's targeting of civilians in terrorist actions.

The film opens with scenes between the French commander Colonel Mathieu and a captured FLN activist that communicate the absolute control of the French and the abject powerlessness of the Algerians, to the strains of Bach-like sacred music. For this role of the Algerian stool pigeon, Sadek, Pontecorvo reportedly was able to arrange for a brief furlough for a petty thief serving a prison sentence; the prisoner was apparently quite upset when he had finished filming his segment and had to return to jail.[7] The presentation of the Algerians as victims is fundamental to the ideological grounding of the film in the writings of Frantz Fanon, the leading theorist of the FLN rebellion. Fanon presents a vision of world history in which racism, violence, and exploitation all emanate from Western colonialism.[8] The historical reality of the Franco-Algerian conflict, however, was that the FLN won the war. Besides those on both sides who perished in the conflict, the losers were the hundreds of thousands of deported *pied noir* French and Algerian civilians, many of whom were by no means rich colonial overlords, but rather humble petite bourgeoisie.[9]

The sequence of the revelation of Ali Le Pointe's hideout by Sadek drifts into a flashback of a panoramic pan of Algiers in 1954, from the European city to the Casbah. Here the film traces the transformation of Ali Le Pointe from petty criminal to nationalist martyr. According to Pontecorvo and Solinas's political precepts, Ali is a character who is emblematic of the manner in which historical forces dominate the lives of individuals. A voice-over of a 1954 FLN communiqué calling the Algerians to arms is read over imagery of Ali as a street hustler performing a three-card monty. When the police arrive, Ali flees, until he is tripped by a young blond Frenchman who in turn receives a brutal punch from Ali. A voice-over lists Ali's record as a petty criminal and past as a boxer, thief, and ruffian. The action shifts to an interior of a prison with inmates playing cards with the interred Ali, reevoking his earlier occupation as a street hustler. Pontecorvo offers a long shot of a prisoner being brought to the guillotine yelling, "Long live Algeria." Ali's curiosity at the reactions of the other prisoners leads him to run to the barred window to witness the execution. An extreme close-up of Ali and a zoom into his eyes accompanies the sound of the guillotine blade falling on the condemned man's neck. With this scene Pontecorvo identifies the moment of Ali's political awakening with the larger historical event of the guillotining of members of FLN in the 1950s.

Besides limiting the film to a specific period that portrays the eventual victors of the conflict as the underdogs, the film, by focusing on Ali as protagonist, imposes a historical vision that undervalues many factors that led to Algerian independence. Political discussions among Algerians in the film are limited to short exchanges between FLN operatives, such as a discussion between Ali and Ben M'hidi, the FLN head, that identifies the ideological rationalization of terrorism as the first step toward leading a popular revolt and gaining attention from the United Nations. In these scenes Ben M'hidi tells Ali that the true difficulties will begin after the revolution. This was the case for the FLN, which suffered a coup in 1965 and would face a de facto civil war with Islamic fundamentalist forces after annulling the results of a 1991 election. By concentrating on a struggle between a nationalist organization like the FLN—which would develop a model of "Algerian socialism" heavily influenced by the the pan-Arab ideology of Egyptian president Gamal Abdel Nasser (1918–1970)—and a French colonial government, the film devalues important players in history of the Franco-Algerian conflict. Pontecorvo has been accused of inadequately mentioning the largest nationalist movement in Algeria, the MNA of Messali Hadj, which existed before the FLN.[10] Pontecorvo and Solinas have responded to this criticism by saying that by the time of the final independence push in Algeria both the Algerian Communist Party and the MNA had been thoroughly compromised and their members absorbed into other factions.[11] But, given subsequent Algerian history, the background of the FLN in the Franco-Algerian conflict is a much more complicated affair than allowed in Pontecorvo's film. There is little mention of the tensions between various Algerian factions within Algeria, nor any mention of the manner in which these conflicts within the proindependence movement spilled over into France among Algerian expatriates during the murderous "café wars." The FLN leaders, largely educated by the French and influenced by Nasser, had adapted concepts of nationalism and socialism to the situation in Algiers. In the film, the cultural division between the educated leader of the FLN, Ben M'hidi, and the former petty criminal Ali Le Pointe is emblematic of the potential cultural conflicts on the Algerian side, since the FLN is led by an elite of committed revolutionaries who must motivate an ignorant, but vigorous, populace (symbolized by Ali Le Pointe) to achieve independence.

A key element of Algerian national identity not adequately emphasized in the film is Islam. The religious component of Algerian and Arab culture has turned out to be a fundamental aspect of later Algerian and Arabic history. As Marxist-influenced intellectuals, Pontecorvo and Solinas assign religion a role secondary to that of economic issues. However, any analysis of Arab and Algerian history in the last decades of the millennium must admit the importance of Islamic fundamentalism in Algerian history, particularly after the annulment of 1991 election, in which the Islamic Salvation Front (FIS) purportedly defeated the FLN, which had led the country to independence and had governed the country under single party rule thereafter. The idea that religious culture could be an important aspect of a national liberation struggle was simply not central to Pontecorvo's ideological mindset when making the film.

The Battle of Algiers does make references to a moral undercurrent in the Franco-Algerian struggle, but these are only fleetingly presented in a context of Islamic identity. When the FLN cell leader Kader tells Ali that the FLN needs to gain public support in the fight against the French, he speaks to Ali about the necessity that the FLN be morally upright and the French be perceived as morally corrupt, as part of the FLN strategy to either convince their opponents or eliminate them. A voice-over citing an FLN communiqué condemning drugs, alcohol, gambling, and prostitution accompanies a scene of Algerian children beating up a drunken Arab man. When Ali returns to his ruffian haunts he smacks opiates from an addict's hands and threatens the pimp who was his mentor, Hacene le Bonois, before shooting him for refusing to accept the FLN's moral dictates. Many of these social vices, in particular the use of alcohol, are specifically prohibited in Islamic codes. But the Islamic nature of these moral attitudes is not emphasized by the filmmaker.

The film does depict a marriage ceremony between two FLN operatives. But the exchange of vows is conducted by an FLN functionary in a lay style that makes evident the secular leanings of the filmmakers and their Algerian coproducers. A voice-over says that the couple is being married by the FLN against the will of the French authorities as an "act of war." The marriage is conducted by an FLN functionary, not a cleric, with the newlyweds signing documents and a limited Muslim prayer as the camera offers a pan over the roofs of the Casbah. The marriage sequence is extremely important because it indicates that Pontecorvo and Solinas visualize a society in which lay authority is predominant and religious sentiment has secondary status. Given the role of Islamic fundamentalism in the country's civil strife following the FLN's annulment of the 1991 elections, the Islamic aspect of the FLN's achievement of independence should not have been presented only as a part of the country's indigenous character, as Pontecorvo has explained in later interviews, but in a wider and more culturally and historically developed context.[12]

Another scene with cultural and religious significance is when FLN women adorn themselves in Western clothes in order to plant bombs among French civilians. Their masquerade is presented as an expedient to pass French checkpoints. The French soldiers afford Algerian women enough respect to allow them to pass a checkpoint unharassed if they assume Western clothing rather than the veils of female Islamic attire. Just as the FLN women bombers masquerade in Western clothes to plant their bombs, Ali and his comrades later disguise themselves in the long robes of Islamic women in order to flee a French dragnet. Ultimately, dress codes are not part of Algerians' affirmation of the moral and cultural aspects of their Islamic identity, but a ruse to avoid detection.

Despite Pontecorvo's seeming devaluation of religion, the film is pregnant with religious imagery at key points in the narrative. After Ali Le Pointe and his comrades are blown up by French forces, Pontecorvo includes a shot of smoke wafting through an archway. The shot could be interpreted in terms of a sacred route awaiting the souls of the martyred nationalist freedom fighters. Rather than shots of the blown-up house and the torn bodies of Ali and his comrades, Pontecorvo offers imagery of otherworldly transcendence, as if the martyred freedom fighters have entered an Algerian nationalist heaven. Before the explosion Pontecorvo offers shots of a praying crowd, so that in the aftermath Ali becomes a de facto religious figure, although Pontecorvo rigorously affords all victims of violence in the film—whether French or Algerian—due respect with sacred music. The scenes of Algerian victims of French torture in particular are accompanied by pathos-evoking sacred music.

The Battle of Algiers also pays little attention to the cultural diversity within Algeria, a country with various tribes as well as rural-urban tensions. In fact, a key element in the FLN's victory was the inability of French forces to maintain control in the rural hinterland of the country, since the ethnic French *pied noir* inhabitants lived mainly in the large city of Algiers. The few scenes depicting the country's French *pied noir* inhabitants precede those in which the FLN women are bombing the malt shop and French airline office.

The one brief speaking role for a *pied noir* character is the appearance of a police commissioner, Henry Arnaud, who complains about the attitude of the central government in Paris intent on maintaining civil liberties which increases the difficulties his commissariat faces as the FLN murders his policemen. Pontecorvo offers an extended montage of FLN murders of police officers, which Arnaud is obviously desperate to stop.

The film's main attempt to depict the mentality of the French inhabitants is when an Arab street sweeper happens to be on a street corner in the European section of town after a montage of the shootings of policemen by FLN guerillas. The street sweeper, Lardjane Boualem, flees from the angry shouts of the *pied noir* inhabitants whose shouts echo the *ratonnade* lynchings concurrent with the FLN independence movement. In the next sequence of the film Arnaud decides to use the man's address on Rue de Thebe as a target for a *pied noir* retaliation, the setting of a bomb in the Casbah. However, in the film the street sweeper is never identified as a member of the FLN. The final cut of the film does not include scenes in the script in which French police beat and torture this street sweeper, and falsely identify him as a police assailant. Thus the choice of the Rue de Thebes address of Boualem, the innocent street sweeper and not an FLN militant, as a target for a *pied noir* bombing is the result of false information. In the next sequences, Arnaud and his comrades leave a swimming pool party, attended by happy French bourgeoisie whose children have Algerian nannies, to plant a bomb at Rue de Thebes, the home of the street sweeper. The placing of the bomb is not presented in the context of the history of the OAS, which also organized mutinies against the French authorities, but merely as a misguided, ill-informed, and callously brutal retaliation. Pontecorvo displays the aftermath of the Casbah bombing in a highly effective manner, with sacred music and scenes of rescuers removing a dead child from a bombed-out building, as the inhabitants search for the bodies of children in the rubble.

Instead of the French *pied noir* inhabitants, the film personifies the French side in the character of head of the French paratroopers, Colonel Mathieu. Pontecorvo and Solinas's first treatment for a film about Algeria, *Para*, had been rejected by Algerian coproducers because the protagonist was a French paratrooper, even though Pontecorvo and Solinas's paratrooper was increasingly disillusioned with his role defending French imperialism. Yet with the character of the French commander Mathieu, the film retains the fascination with the studied machismo of the French professional soldier from *Para*. The original treatment for *Para* makes much of the main character's physical attractiveness. Pontecorvo intended to cast Paul Newman or Warren Beatty, then in their physical prime as Hollywood leading men, in the leading role in *Para*. This current is retained in *The Battle of Algiers*, in which Mathieu, played

Jean Martin (Colonel Mathieu) leads a parade of
French paratroopers in The Battle of Algiers. *Courtesy of Photofest*

by Jean Martin, is supposed to cut a dashing figure. The Mathieu character is to be a combination of a number of historical figures, including the historical head of the French paratroopers in Algiers, Jacques Massu, and Marcel Bigeard, a figure active in the French army units fighting on the Allied side in World War II before serving in Algeria.[13] The fictional Colonel Mathieu's résumé includes experience in the French resistance, Italy, and Indochina and a degree in engineering from a prestigious French university, the Ecole Polytechnique. Mathieu's résumé makes him an iconic manifestation of the presumptive professionalism of the French military, which critics have noted as an element of objectivity in the film.[14] According to this interpretation, despite the fact that Pontecorvo is evidently supportive of the national liberation struggle of the Algerians, he portrays the main French character as a largely sympathetic figure.[15] In fact in the film Mathieu is not just a soldier, but a representative of European and Western civilization. However, by attempting to present the French leader as an educated and cultured person, the film actually rationalizes the atrocities and torture that Mathieu authorizes. In the film torture is the exclusive territory of the French, whereas historically the denial of human rights through torture was practiced by both sides. But like Arnaud, the

pied noir police commissioner who plants a bomb in the Casbah, killing innocent civilians, Mathieu displays inadequate moral introspection about his orders to murder and torture potentially innocent detainees. He subordinates
ethics to his interpretation of the practical concern of gaining information to
destroy the FLN network. Mathieu falls back on his code as a military man
and deflects journalists' queries about his methods by questioning the motivations and the resolve of the French nation, which sent troops to quash the rebellion in the first place. Mathieu even upbraids the journalists who dare to insult his troops by referring to them as Nazis or Fascists by informing them that
some of the French soldiers were survivors of Nazi concentration camps at
Dachau and Buchenwald.

   The characterization of Mathieu may be ascribed to the screenwriters' deterministic vision of history, in which the characters in the film are not just individuals but manifestations of larger historical forces, a narrative current that recalls the scripts of *La grande strada azzurra/The Wide Blue Road* and *Kapò*.
Mathieu complains about laws that impede his actions and he rationalizes the
use of torture by explaining to the press corps that the FLN requests that its operatives to withhold information for twenty-four hours in order to allow the organization time to anticipate French reprisals. He describes the pyramidal structure of the FLN, in which each operative only knows the name of two other
members, and compares the FLN to a tapeworm that will regrow unless the
head is removed. Despite the director's attempts to portray Mathieu as a sympathetic figure, his actions cannot be viewed as anything except hypocritical and in-
consistent in someone who is presumably well educated and fought in the anti-
Nazi/Fascist resistance. Mathieu's arrogant rationalizations for the use of torture
rely on a short-run argument that since he is aware of the pyramidal structure of
the FLN, torture is used to gain specific information—the names of the two operatives that each member of the FLN knows. In fact Mathieu's methods are effective in the short run, since he is victorious in his mission of quelling the rebellion in the city of Algiers. But since the French victory in the Battle of Algiers
occurs in the larger context of their defeat in the Franco-Algerian War, the
French use of torture, and the filmmakers' depiction of torture as exclusively
French, takes on a larger meaning. The use of barbaric methods by French forces
ultimately diminishes their prestige and makes the sympathetic portrayal of
Mathieu an ironic metaphor for the inability of the French to preserve the ideals
of civilization and the sanctity of civil rights, which they claim to represent.

   The exchanges between Mathieu and the captured Algerian leader Ben
M'hidi before the latter dies mysteriously in prison seem like a debate between intellectuals in European salons, with mutual manifestations of respect and *politesse*. Both leaders rationalize their own use of violence and
murder by pointing out the crimes of their counterpart rather than accept-

Shootout between French paratroopers and disguised FLN guerillas led by
Ali Le Pointe. Courtesy of Photofest

ing their own culpability. When Mathieu in exasperation responds to a journalist's question about the criticism of the war by existentialist philosopher
Jean Paul Sartre, Mathieu's comment begs an analysis beyond the intentions
of the filmmakers. Mathieu's question, "Why are the Sartres always on the
other side?" is paradoxical, since many French intellectuals of Sartre's generation were not particularly known for their activity in the French resistance
against the Nazi-Vichy government. A rigorous ethical/philosophical stance
on the Franco-Algerian war would have been critical of the violence used by
both sides.

Actually, the displays of mutual respect between the Algerian nationalist
Ali Ben M'hidi and the French nationalist Mathieu may be explained by the
realization that they have much in common. Each wants to impose a language, religion, culture, dress, and sexual code on the other. *The Battle of Algiers* takes the position that the oppressed nationalistic impulses of the indigenous M'hidi are more justifiable than those of the French colonialist and
nationalist Mathieu. The aspiration for independence and self-determination
is more legitimate than the drive for imperial dominion. But in a larger context the film defers personal responsibility for crimes committed by both sides
due to their essence as pawns in a larger historical process. Both the terrorist

armed struggle of the Algerians and the attempts at repressing an independence movement by resorting to torture of the French military are presented
as historical necessities; where the players involved do not display the ethical
resolve to act outside larger historical process. Violence, whether by Mathieu's
paratroopers or Le Pointe's FLN operatives, ultimately denies the basic human dignity of innocent victims who suffer for nationalistic political objec-
tives, whether French or Algerian. The ultimate message of the film is that a
willingness to resort to violence bestows and reinforces political legitimacy.
Ali Le Pointe's violence leads to the independence of Algeria but also to the
murder of civilians and the deportation of the French *pied noirs*. One of the
historical ironies of FLN attacks, as might be expected in a civil conflict, was
that according to some reports they resulted in more Algerian than French
victims.[16] Mathieu's violence leads to the temporary pacification of the city of
Algiers at the cost of the torture and murder of Algerians. The actions of both
the French troops and the Algerian insurgents deny the human rights of their
victims and are morally reprehensible in a larger ethical context.[17] The ultimate result of the Algerian struggle for independence was the replacement of
a French colonial elite with the Algerian FLN, which sowed the seeds for the
next phase of civil strife in Algeria. This next phase became apparent when
the FLN annulled the 1991 elections and a de facto civil war began, with the
number of victims rivaling that of the Franco-Algerian war of the late 1950s.
Given the successive rapprochement between France and Algeria since independence, *The Battle of Algiers* could be read as documenting not only the re-
moval of colonial oppression and the attainment of national identity, but also
the manner in which violence spreads and denies human dignity to the detri-
ment of a collective whole.

Mathieu's press conferences anticipate the media hype that terrorist violence excites to the present day. The film depicts the fascination with violence
in the court of world opinion, which learns about events in Algiers through a
media filter. The cool, detached macho figure of Mathieu, the Paul Muni–like
Kader, the Pépé le Moko–like Ali Le Pointe, and the Algerian bomb setter
wearing dark sunglasses like a beatnik poet as he sets the timers for the FLN
women bombers are all figures who emanate a brutal appeal. The adolescent
one-upmanship of violent acts by both sides panders to audiences' voyeuristic
impulses. If the film is to have continuing relevance in the decades to come—
and, given the persistence of terrorism as a political tool worldwide, such a
destiny for *The Battle of Algiers* seems certain—then the film must also be recognized for the manner in which it rationalizes the use of violence as a political tool, whether clandestine or state sponsored.

As mentioned, the film's unwitting rationalization of violence may be
proven by the fact that it actually has two endings. One ending validates the

oppressive means used by Mathieu's French paratroopers to break the rebellion. In these last scenes, Mathieu appears after the French paratroopers have trapped and blown up Ali Le Pointe and his comrades in the Casbah. But the film also has a coda in which Mathieu does not appear, and the efforts of FLN militants like Ali Le Pointe and Kader result in the development of a collective consciousness among the Algerian populace that leads to the popular uprising that effectively evicts the French. Thus both Ali Le Pointe and Mathieu exit the film as victors. Ali is victorious since his efforts lead to the eviction of the French. Mathieu is victorious since he completes his mission and quells the Casbah revolt of the FLN. In this context the reduction of the ethical/religious aspects of the Algerian struggle to a secondary, even folkloristic, role is the Achilles heel of the film. It deprives the film of an ethical grounding at a higher level than the pan-Arabic nationalism of the Nasserite FLN or the arrogant assumption of France's civilizing mission according to the nationalist precepts of Gaullist France. The film's current and continued popularity among both terrorist organizations and state counterinsurgency units may be explained by its vivid and convincing depiction of the use of violence by both sides, the national liberation terrorists of the FLN and the French counterinsurgent colonialists.[18]

If *The Battle of Algiers* has flaws in its historical re-creation, what it does brilliantly is re-create the vibrancy of the Italian neorealist documentary style. But if the film is a triumph in terms of style it does not achieve neorealist standards in terms of narrative. One of Pontecorvo's models for the film was undeniably Rossellini's *Roma città aperta/Rome Open City* (1945). There are too many thematic similarities between the two films for the connection to be casual.[19] Both films feature forces of oppression (the Nazis in *Rome Open City* and the French in *The Battle of Algiers*) attempting to suppress activists of a freedom-fighting resistance (Don Pietro and Manfredi in *Rome Open City* and Ali Le Pointe and Kader in *The Battle of Algiers*). Both films are stories of defeats of clandestine operations that were eventually victorious in the overall conflict. But the characterizations in *Rome Open City* cast a wider net and give a more complete idea of historical events in occupied Rome during World War II than Pontecorvo's film does for Algiers in the late 1950s. The great neorealist films, like Rossellini's *Rome Open City* or Vittorio De Sica's *Ladri di biciclette/The Bicycle Thief*, were remarkably able to condense and re-create entire historical cycles into brief vignettes and characterizations. Rossellini's *Rome Open City* gives a fairly intricate picture of Rome before Allied liberation, with characters who succinctly communicate much wider historical discourses. In *Rome Open City* the German Gestapo commander Bergman puts the ability of partisan fighter Manfredi to resist in terms of the racism of Nazi ideology. Hartmann, the German veteran of World War I, goes on a drunken tirade in which he decries how the violent efforts of his nation have reaped only a harvest of hatred. The question of Italian war guilt and collaboration is skirted in the scene of the Italian firing squad that purposefully misses Don Pietro and the subservience of the Italian police commissioner and army officers collaborating with the Nazis. The Italian women who consort with German troops have clear, if shallow, motivations. Manfredi, the communist activist and veteran of the Spanish Civil War, works with the Catholic priest, Don Pietro, for the common anti-Nazi/Fascist cause, with specific mentions of the Italian government in exile and the Committee of National Liberation (CLN), which unified resistance factions. Above all, the character of Don Pietro represents the Catholic cultural essence of Italy, and the ending of the film—in which a group of boys who have witnessed Don Pietro's execution walk into a backdrop of St. Peter's basilica—alludes to the political future of postwar Italy, which would be dominated by political parties aligned with Catholicism.

The Battle of Algiers does anticipate some events in later Algerian history. The FLN would rule the country as a single-party governing body during the postindependence period. But Pontecorvo's characters are vehicles for the sort of deterministic historical vision that recalls his earlier films *The Wide Blue Road* and *Kapò*. As stated, *The Battle of Algiers* omits important aspects of the history of the Algerian revolt, such as the rural war, the OAS, the mutiny of French troops after initial accords were reached with the FLN, the various factions within the Algerian rebellion, and, most importantly, the Islamic undercurrent of the revolt so central to subsequent Algerian history. Pontecorvo's repeated use of voice-overs of communiqués from the FLN high command and the last voice-over, indicating the ignorance of FLN leaders in exile about the final popular revolt, do not reach the narrative quality of characterizations in the neorealist canon of films by Rossellini or De Sica. The emphasis of *The Battle of Algiers* is the process through which Ali Le Pointe gains a sense of revolutionary consciousness and becomes a nationalist martyr as a figure who is a pawn of larger historical forces. But the larger issues of the moral ramifications of violence and war guilt are not treated in Pontecorvo's re-creation of occupied Algiers with the same depth as in Rossellini's film about occupied Rome. Rossellini's *Rome Open City* places the violence of the war into a religious and ethical context with little of the rationalization present in *The Battle of Algiers*. The violence of the actual events that inspired *Rome Open City*—the bombing of a Nazi column in Via Rasella and the subsequent Nazi retaliation with mass executions at the *fosse ardeatine*—are attenuated, as the use of violence by partisans takes a secondary thematic role to the message of spiritual responsibility delivered by the protagonist of the film, the Roman Catholic priest Don Pietro.

Part of the thematic strategy of *The Battle of Algiers* may be of a carnival-like process that is part of political revolution.[20] The narrative depends on the contrast between the illiterate ex-criminal Ali Le Pointe, an Algerian from the lowest strata of society, and the hypereducated and much-decorated Colonel Mathieu. In the film what is lowly and abject is raised and what is high and mighty is brought down to earth, as Le Pointe becomes powerful enough to lead a rebellion that would eventually defeat the nation that Mathieu represents. The film is replete with episodes of masquerade and role reversal. The film opens with scenes of the Algerian informer Sadek dressed as a French paratrooper and revealing Ali Le Pointe's final hideout in the Casbah. When the FLN gives Ali an empty gun and orders him to shoot a French policeman as a test of loyalty, the exercise is presented as a carnival-like joke. Petit Omar even offers Ali a carnival-like, role reversal message: "Men have two faces, one which laughs and one which cries." Before shooting the policeman, Ali makes a triumphant declaration about the role reversal to the prone policeman, which is then reversed again, since his gun is not loaded. In another scene of role reversals a gang of small children beat and abuse a drunken Algerian man who should dominate them. Carnival imagery extends to the Algerian women who masquerade as Westerners and seem to fraternize with French troops at a checkpoint in order to bring death and destruction by planting bombs among dancing teenagers at a milk bar or tourists at the French airline office. In the final sequences Ali and Kader dress in the full-length veils of Islamic women in order to avoid a French dragnet. Role reversals and carnival-like imagery are central to the film, which is about how a third world country, Algeria, defeats a declining colonial power, France.

Besides drawing from the historical determinism and the stylistic reevocation of Italian neorealism, the film draws from Hollywood gangster films. In narrative terms the film is a contest between Ali Le Pointe as the hiding outlaw and Mathieu as the crusading policeman who controls the city from his office. This story line is not only repeated from Rossellini's *Rome Open City* but also from Julien Duvivier's gangster film *Pépé le Moko* (1937) starring Jean Gabin, which was in turn heavily influenced by Hollywood gangster films of the 1930s such as *Little Caesar* (1930) with Edgar G. Robinson, *The Public Enemy* (1931) with James Cagney, and *Scarface* (1932) with Paul Muni.[21] Thus the urban underworld labyrinth of Chicago streets that hides Edgar G. Robinson's character in *Little Caesar* or Paul Muni's character in *Scarface* becomes the Casbah for Jean Gabin in *Pépé le Moko* and Brahim Haggiag as Ali Le Pointe in *The Battle of Algiers*. That Pontecorvo organized the film according to this urban narrative model is paradoxical due to the actual historical course of events, in which the French actually lost control of the country in the countryside, where there were fewer French *pied noir* colonists.

There has also been an undeniable if unexamined influence of *The Battle of Algiers* on commercial cinema, including Hollywood. The influence of

Pontecorvo's work on films like Steven Spielberg's *Schindler's List* (1993), which like *Kapò* deals with the Holocaust, and *Amistad* (1997), which like *Burn!* deals with slavery, is apparent.[22] But there is also an unrecognized echo of *The Battle of Algiers* in George Lucas's *Star Wars* (1979), a film that has enough elements in common with Pontecorvo's film to support an argument that *Star Wars* is a veiled remake of *The Battle of Algiers*. *Star Wars* features a humble underdog, Luke Skywalker, who is mentored by the wise Ben Obi-Wan Kenobi, two characters with marked similarities to the roles of Ali Le Pointe and his mentor Ben M'hidi in *The Battle of Algiers*. Both M'hidi and Obi-Wan Kenobi regale their inexperienced charges with speeches about self-less missions. The ephemeral "force" of the *Star Wars* Jedi cult could be read as the heir to the national liberation ideology of the FLN. There are also similarities between the antagonists in the films. Both Mathieu and Darth Vader are figures working for an empire who in the past struggled on the side of the oppressed. Just as Vader is a fallen Jedi knight who has succumbed to the "dark side" of the force, Mathieu is a veteran of the fight against Nazi/Vichy forces in World War II who has become a paladin of oppressive French imperialism. Certain sequences in *Star Wars* seem to take direct influence from *The Battle of Algiers*, such as the sequence of Ali Le Pointe's visit to a bar, which recalls the bar scene in *Star Wars* and has a similar fight. Both films have imperial paratroopers manning checkpoints and rebels who invent clever ruses in order to evade detection. *Star Wars* opens in the desertlike setting of Luke Skywalker's home planet, whose inhabitants, the Sand People, have a dress and appearance with Arabian elements. Skywalker's planet also has a cityscape with a Casbah-like labyrinth that recalls the Algiers of *The Battle of Algiers*. Each protagonist even has a miniscule sidekick adept at evading and ridiculing imperial soldiers: Ali is accompanied by Little Omar, and Luke Skywalker has the robot R2D2. Both films also have themes of the use of violence against innocent civilians to further political aims. Vader's Death Star obliterates an entire rebellious planet as a lesson to others planning revolts. A major difference is that the rebels in *Star Wars* do not target civilians like the FLN of *The Battle of Algiers*.

Pontecorvo's *The Battle of Algiers* is a seminal film in cinema history. Pontecorvo's masterful re-creation of the vibrancy of the Italian neorealist style has unfortunately not been widely followed despite the film's commercial and critical success. It is hard to understand why there have been so few films about the numerous historical events since the Franco-Algerian war that have commanded a re-creation of the proto-neorealist approach adopted by Pontecorvo in *The Battle of Algiers*. If *The Battle of Algiers* has not had many followers in political cinema, it has had a remarkable, if unexamined, influence on "third cinema," the emerging cinemas of developing countries.

The Battle of Algiers has gained a renewed relevance due to the persistent plague of politically motivated terrorism worldwide. The murder of civilians by the militants of the FLN and the OAS during the Franco-Algerian war, as depicted in the film, with the first targeting of civilians by nonstate organizations, was disseminated by a modern, international press corps, with international public opinion coming to bear on the ultimate outcome of the conflict. Pontecorvo's portrayal of these events with an ideological slant dependent on the writings of cultural theorists like Frantz Fanon makes *The Battle of Algiers* a film that was very much a product of its time, in which the worldwide struggle by countries to remove the yoke of colonialism had such an immediate resonance. In the early 1960s many countries throughout the world were ending colonial domination and experiencing their first taste of domestic rule, as the European colonial empires steadily granted autonomy to their former colonial holdings, whether through force or negotiation. As in *Kapò*, Pontecorvo tackled a subject with vast resonance and immediate pertinence in world history and had a chance to apply his political outlook and personal experiences in the Italian resistance of World War II. But as *The Battle of Algiers* has gained renewed relevance due to the rise of Islamic terrorism, and the events depicted have lost their immediacy, the film has become a source for the training of both the Right and the Left.[23] The filmmaker presented the Franco-Algerian conflict as a national liberation and anticolonial struggle, but as the film acquires a new context in the postcolonial period, what remains of the film is the impression that violence legitimizes itself due to the courage needed to unleash it and that torture may be rationalized if it has the goal of attaining information for the immediate prevention of an attack. As any motivated minority has learned in the era of political terrorism, the use of violence is a key tactic adopted by movements attempting to gain political legitimacy, and torture is a tool used by counterinsurgency organizations with the goal of attaining information to prevent violence. The film is a convincing portrayal of both a clandestine armed struggle and its repression by an effective state-sponsored counterinsurgency. But the film ultimately has a Machiavellian essence regarding the use of violence, where the results of violence carry more weight than ethical concerns, and where the ultimate goal of the perpetrators of violence should be to inspire fear rather than hatred or disdain among the populace. The film's dual ending, depicting victories for both the French and the Algerians, actually avoids the larger question of the ethical legitimacy of violence as a political tool. This is an issue that Pontecorvo would be forced to face in his last feature film, *Ogro* (1979), and in the documentary that chronicles Pontecorvo's return to an Algeria on the brink of civil war with Islamic fundamentalism in 1991, *Gillo Pontecorvo's Return to Algiers* (1992).

NOTES

1. Irene Bignardi, *Memorie estorte a uno smemorato vita di Gillo Pontecorvo* (Milan: Feltrinelli, 1999).

2. Bignardi, *Memorie.*

3. Bignardi, *Memorie.*

4. Luigi Cipriani, M. Conciatori, M. Giraldi, and L. Ricci, eds., *Primo piano sull'autore Gillo Pontecorvo "La dittatura della verità"* (Rome: Designer, 1999), 30.

5. Antonio Musu, "Interview with Musu," *The Battle of Algiers,* DVD (Rome: DNC Home Entertainment, 2003).

6. Gillo Pontecorvo, *"The Battle of Algiers:* An Adventure in Filming," *American Cinematographer* (April 1967): 266–69.

7. Gillo Pontecorvo, "Interview," *The Battle of Algiers,* DVD (Rome: DNC Home Entertainment, 2003).

8. Frantz Fanon, *A Dying Colonialism,* trans. Haakon Chevalier (New York: Grove, 1965); Philip Dine, *Images of the Algerian War: French Fiction and Film, 1954–1992* (Oxford: Claredon, 1994).

9. Giorgio Allorio, "Interview," *The Battle of Algiers,* DVD (Rome: DNC Home Entertainment, 2003).

10. Joan Mellen, *Filmguide to "The Battle of Algiers"* (Bloomington: Indiana University Press, 1973), 62.

11. Franco Solinas, *Gillo Pontecorvo's "The Battle of Algiers": A Film Written by Franco Solinas,* ed. Pier Nico (New York: Scribner, 1973), 197.

12. Edward Said, "The Dictatorship of Truth: An Interview with Gillo Pontecorvo," *Cineaste* 25, no. 2 (2000): 25.

13. Jacques Massu, *La vraie bataille d'Alger* (Paris: Plon, 1971).

14. Joan Mellen, *Filmguide to "The Battle of Algiers"* (Bloomington: Indiana University Press, 1973), 62.

15. Robert Stam and Ella Shohat, *Unthinking Eurocentrism: Multiculturalism and the Media* (New York: Routledge, 1994), 253.

16. Martha Crenshaw, "The Causes of Terrorism," *Comparative Politics* 13, no. 4 (July 1981): 379–99.

17. Giorgio Allorio, "Interview," *The Battle of Algiers,* DVD (Rome: DNC Home Entertainment, 2003).

18. Stuart Klawans, "Lessons of the Pentagon's Favorite Training Film," *New York Times,* January 4, 2004, 26.

19. While I was unable to find the original source of the reference to Pontecorvo's debt to Rossellini, given Pontecorvo's numerous statements about his debt to *Rome Open City,* the idea of a connection between *The Battle of Algiers* and *Rome Open City* has become a critical commonplace.

20. Mikhail Bakhtin, *Rabelais and His World,* trans. Helene Iswolsky (Bloomington: Indiana University Press, 1984).

21. Ginette Vincendeau, *Pépé le Moko* (London: BFI, 1998).

22. Charlie Glass, "The Hour of the Birth of Death: Pontecorvo's Long Silence and the Demise of Political Film-making," *Times Literary Supplement,* June 28, 1998, 21.

23. Stuart Klawans, "Lessons of the Pentagon's Favorite Training Film," *New York Times,* January 4, 2004, 26.

· 6 ·

The Colonial, Postcolonial Parable of
Queimada!/Burn! (1969)

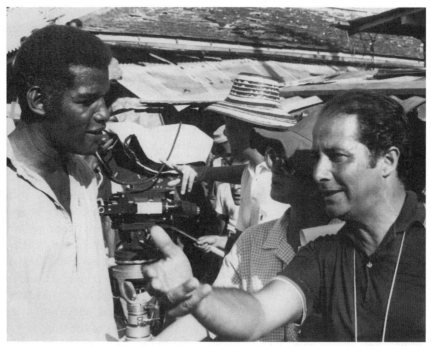

Pontecorvo instructing Evaristo Márquez (Josè Dolores) in Burn! *Courtesy of Photofest*

*A*fter the international success of *La battaglia di Algeri/The Battle of Algiers*, which earned Pontecorvo his second nomination for an Academy Award, Pontecorvo began another search for a project. Alberto Grimaldi, the producer of Sergio Leone's western trilogy starring Clint Eastwood,[1] was interested in hiring Pontecorvo to direct a script by Franco Solinas, who had been active penning scripts for a number of political westerns: *La resa dei conti/The Big Gundown* (1966), *¿Quien sabe?/A Bullet for the General* (1967) by Damiano Damiani, and *Tepepa . . . Viva la revolución/Long Live the Revolution* (1968). Grimaldi had commissioned an adaptation of a Guy de Maupassant story, *Bel ami*, to be set in Mexico at the beginning of the century and entitled *Il Mercenario/The Mercenary* (1968), from Solinas and Giorgio Arlorio. The topic had a political message that seemed made to order for Pontecorvo. However, *The Mercenary*, eventually directed by Sergio Corbucci, would be another of the worthy projects that Pontecorvo would refuse. Despite Pontecorvo's rejection of *The Mercenary*, Solinas and Grimaldi continued to approach him about making a western, a genre that had gained a new relevance in the late 1960s. Grimaldi hoped to continue on the path of Sergio Leone, who with *C'era una volta il West/Once upon a Time in the West* (1968) had taken the western to new thematic and box office territory, casting Henry Fonda—usually chosen for heroic roles like the lead in John Ford's *Young Mr. Lincoln* (1939) or Wyatt Earp in *My Darling Clementine* (1946)—against type as a child-murdering outlaw.[2] In Leone's revision the American West was not only the epic setting of the formation of the United States, but a mélange of rampaging commercial interests, racial and class tensions, and above all, violence.

Pontecorvo had been tempted to make a film about the incident later used by Dario Fo for his play *Morte accidentale di un anarchico/Accidental Death of an Anarchist*. But after the success of *The Battle of Algiers*, and with the political climate charged by the American war in Vietnam, Pontecorvo remained interested in the processes of colonialism, which he has subsequently called the "matrix of our entire civilization."[3] Pontecorvo, Solinas, Alorio, and producer Grimaldi finally decided to make an action adventure film with American producers at United Artists. By the late 1960s Pontecorvo, who was born in 1919, was pushing fifty, married with a family. Pecuniary concerns began to gain importance in his life. It was in this period, in fact, that Pontecorvo was tempted by offers to make television commercials and industrial documentaries, activities that would help support his family, since he made so few films as a director of features.[4] Pontecorvo was initially averse to working in a popular genre like the western. Eventually, Pontecorvo agreed to adapt the format of the historical action adventure film to issues of the third world and colonialism, an idea that Grimaldi accepted in his eagerness to work with Pontecorvo after the financial and critical success of *The Battle of Algiers*. The fact that Pontecorvo made so few films actually seems to have increased his cachet among producers and actors.

Pontecorvo became aware of the life of American adventurer William Walker (1824–1860) from reading about him in the *Encyclopedia Britannica*. Walker was born in Tennessee and educated as a doctor and lawyer, but in

1853 he became an international adventurer by invading Baja California with a band of committed followers. Walker was able to proclaim himself president of the short-lived republic of Baja California and Sonora before surrendering to U.S. authorities. In 1855 Walker repeated the escapade with an invasion of Nicaragua, where he was inaugurated president in 1856. Walker apparently planned to create a wider union of Central American countries under his authority, but was thwarted by American tycoon Cornelius Vanderbilt after Walker's followers seized some of Vanderbilt's assets during the Nicaragua scheme. With Vanderbilt's aid, Walker was overthrown in 1857, captured by the British, and executed in Honduras in 1860.[5]

Through the story of the historical William Walker, Pontecorvo became interested in the period of the early nineteenth century in which adventurers had been able to mold the world through personal audacity. In Pontecorvo's film *Queimada!/Burn!* the historical adventurer William Walker becomes Sir William Walker, an agent first of the British Foreign Office and then the transnational Royal Sugar Company. Pontecorvo's aim in the film was to present the roots of colonialism in a manner that borrowed heavily from Solinas's interest in English adventure novels of the nineteenth century and authors like Joseph Conrad (1857–1924) and Rudyard Kipling (1865–1936), as well as from the *Corto Maltese* comic book series by Hugo Pratt. The film was to have as a theoretical underpinning the work of authors like Frantz Fanon.[6] Apparently the first versions of the script even retained some of the flashback structure found in the English adventure novels of Conrad, like *Heart of Darkness*, and Kipling's short story *The Man Who Would Be King*.[7]

Pontecorvo's determined nature did not serve him as well on *Burn!* as it had on previous projects. On *Burn!* Pontecorvo would be responsible to producers and a star, Marlon Brando, who despite enormous displays of patience were not willing to defer to Pontecorvo's will indefinitely and uncritically. American producers were convinced by Grimaldi that Pontecorvo would provide a film like Leone's Italian spaghetti westerns, which were profitable in the late 1960s. Yet true to his nature, Pontecorvo wanted to make a film according to his political and artistic vision. Considering the scope of the project, Pontecorvo was actually allowed an astonishing amount of freedom on *Burn!* particularly as compared to the working conditions of directors in subsequent generations. The experience for Pontecorvo was actually his first contact with the commercial machinery of a Hollywood studio, United Artists, which banked on Pontecorvo's name and prestige after his Academy Award nominations for *Kapò* and *The Battle of Algiers*. Pontecorvo, whose experience was limited to the Italian film industry and some assistant directing in France during the mid-1950s, has stated that he found the trappings of a Hollywood production to be an enormous and overbearing responsibility.[8]

Marlon Brando (Sir William Walker) in Burn! *Courtesy of Photofest*

Pontecorvo and Solinas actually began the project with the idea that Marlon Brando would be perfect to play the British agent, William Walker. American studio executives had generously suggested Steve McQueen, a top male box office draw in 1968. McQueen was fresh from his role in Robert Wise's *The Sand Pebbles* (1966) as an American sailor in the midst of upheavals in turn-of-the-century China.[9] Pontecorvo insisted on Brando, who had seen *The Battle of Algiers* and made statements reproduced in the press that the one European director he would like to work with was Pontecorvo. In the late 1960s Brando's career was at a bit of a standstill. His films before *Burn!* had not performed well at the box office. In *Burn!* Brando would play an individual suited to a life of action who is faced with a moral dilemma, a role recalling his previous films *On the Waterfront* (1954), *One Eyed Jacks* (1960), *Mutiny on the Bounty* (1962), and *The Ugly American* (1963).

Despite not being allowed to film in black and white, Pontecorvo was able to remain true to his neorealist roots by casting a large number of non-professionals in leading roles. Pontecorvo had discovered Brahim Haggiag, who played Ali Le Pointe in *The Battle of Algiers*, on the streets of Algiers; he also cast Evaristo Marquez, a local he found riding a horse in the interior of Columbia, as Josè Dolores in *Burn!* Like Haggiag, Marquez was illiterate and had no background in the cinema or the acting profession. Marquez was signed based on Pontecorvo's guarantee of his suitability to the American producers. The executives at United Artists had proposed Sidney Poitier, the premier black male actor in Hollywood at the time, for the role of the ex-slave turned rebel leader Josè Dolores. Pontecorvo's has claimed that he rejected Poitier because he wanted a savage face and not the civilized New York visage of a well-known actor like Poitier.[10] Brando was reportedly so interested in working with Pontecorvo that he accepted the role without reading the script and subsequently agreed to costar with the unknown Evaristo Marquez based solely on Pontecorvo's assurances that Marquez was suitable for the role of Josè Dolores opposite Brando as the protagonist, Walker.[11]

Thus, on the surface the cast for *Burn!* allowed Pontecorvo the best of both worlds. He cast an absolute nonprofessional in a leading role, in the tradition of Vittorio De Sica's casting of Lamberto Maggiorani in *Ladri di biciclette/The Bicycle Thief*. But he also had one of the premier actors of the Hollywood cinema in Marlon Brando. The character of Josè Dolores, like that of Ali Le Pointe in *The Battle of Algiers*, would be a vehicle for the message that Pontecorvo and Solinas intended for the film—their Marxist and deterministic theory that historical processes are more dominant than individual initiative.

Evaristo Marquez (Josè Dolores) left, and Marlon Brando (Sir William Walker) right, in Burn! *Courtesy of Photofest*

The raw authenticity of the nonprofessional Evaristo Marquez would thus play against the professionalism and charisma of Brando. Other members of the cast were also nonprofessional actors. The English ambassador, Mr. Shelton, is played by Norman Hill, an Englishman who worked for Shell Oil Company in Colombia. Since *Burn!* features Marlon Brando as William Walker and veteran Italian actor Renato Salvatori as Teddy Sanchez, the film offers an interesting mix of professionals and nonprofessionals.[12]

Pontecorvo's preference for nonprofessionals could be interpreted as a result of his memories of his own appearance as a nonprofessional novice as the partisan guerilla Pietro in Aldo Vergano's World War II resistance drama *Outcry*. Pontecorvo directed his first feature film, *La grande strada azzurra/The Wide Blue Road*, using two actors, Alida Valli and Yves Montand, who had much more experience than he did. Despite Pontecorvo's attempts, the performances in the *The Wide Blue Road* did not reach the level of sincerity that Pontecorvo sought as a filmmaker coming out of the Italian neorealist tradition. *Kapò* was similarly conditioned by a professional stage actress, Susan Strasberg, and the established French actress Emmanuele Riva; their performances also did not communicate the authenticity of the neorealist style. Pontecorvo attained excellent results with the nonprofessionals in *The Battle of Algiers* and justifiably sought to continue in that vein in *Burn!*

Filming was characterized by the argumentative atmosphere created by Pontecorvo, his American producers, and above all the star of the film, Marlon Brando, who began the film full of anticipation for the directorial brilliance of Pontecorvo. However, like the American producers, Brando was increasingly alienated by Pontecorvo over the course of the production. Brando had initially been totally deferent to Pontecorvo's wishes, but difficulties arose as the crew had to adapt to the inexperience of Marquez, who was costarring in the film as Josè Dolores. The untrained Columbian actor reportedly had extreme difficulty conveying specific emotions on command. These problems were initially overcome by Pontecorvo with directing tricks that recall those of the neorealist tradition. For example, Pontecorvo had Marquez look down and then lift his head in order to convey the emotion of irony.[13] One scheme that Pontecorvo and Brando devised was for Marquez to watch Brando's face as the camera shot him from behind Brando's back and then copy the expression on Brando's face. Eventually, Brando tired of these tricks and, more importantly, became increasingly uncomfortable with Pontecorvo's directing style, to the point that in the course of the production the two had to speak through an intermediary. Brando and Pontecorvo reportedly did not even shake hands after the film was completed.[14] Brando was not accustomed to a director stubbornly refusing to accept ideas about scenes. Despite Pontecorvo's generous political views about collectivity in his earlier films, when it came to his own territory on a film set he was stubbornly fixed in a mindset that emanated from the European auteurist tradition; according to this mindset, the film should be the mirror of the defects and the abilities of a single person, the film's director.[15] Stories of quarreling between Brando and Pontecorvo and the alleged forty-one takes Pontecorvo had demanded for a single scene (Brando claimed the number was forty-eight) filtered through to the press and disillusioned the film's American backers, who never advertised and distributed the film in the manner it deserved. United Artists retained a contractual right to do a final edit, for which they hired an American producer, Andy Kuehn, who reportedly cut Pontecorvo's version by twenty-five minutes for the North American print.[16] The film was released worldwide but did not perform well outside Italy and became a professional setback for Brando and particularly for Pontecorvo, whose creative career never recovered.

The conflict between Brando and Pontecorvo was actually a clash of cinematic cultures. Pontecorvo, trained in the neorealist idea of improvisation, had an approach to acting that was the antithesis of Brando's background in method acting. Pontecorvo had already encountered difficulties with method actress Susan Strasberg on *Kapò*; he reportedly instructed assistant director Giuliano Montaldo to slap the actress and humiliate her in front of the crew in order to film her as she burst into tears. Pontecorvo later commented that Brando's style of method acting, so dependent on the ability of an actor to recreate the mindset of a character, was more suited for a theatrical venue and the few scenes in films in which psychological introspection is important. Pontecorvo, who reportedly communicated with Brando in French, had difficulty responding to Brando's repeated questions about the state of mind of the Walker character. As a director, Pontecorvo was often more aware of the physical aspects of the set than the concerns of an individual actor, even if the actor was of Brando's caliber.[17]

Brando also came to disapprove of the conditions and heat of Pontecorvo's choice of set location, the city of Cartagena in Columbia. Cartagena was a former Spanish colonial city whose architecture had changed little since the nineteenth century and whose inhabitants were an ethnic mix well suited to the story line of a Caribbean island with a large population of African descent. After reportedly receiving kidnapping threats, Brando eventually succeeded in relocating the production from Cartagena to Morocco. The story and title of the film were also changed, so that the historical setting became a Portuguese colony, Queimada, rather than a Spanish colony, Quemada. The government of Spain under Dictator Francisco Franco protested that the film would negatively portray Spanish colonial forces. There was a precedent of an American studio suffering repercussions from Franco's disapproval: the Franco regime had threatened to refuse permissions for the distribution of an

American studio's products in Spain following the release of Fred Zinnemann's film *Behold a Pale Horse* (1964), a Spanish Civil War tale.[18]

Burn! may be analyzed according to the intentions of the screenwriters, Arlorio and Solinas, and the director, Pontecorvo, to make a film about the origins of colonialism and the subsequent transition from traditional colonialism to a neocolonial model in which commercial interests retain control over the natural resources of a third world country, with nominal control by an indigenous oligarchy. Walker's speeches to the island elite or even to rebel leader Josè Dolores paraphrase the cultural theories of writers like Frantz Fanon or summarize statements about guerilla warfare tactics from nationalist leaders like Ho Chi Minh or Mao Tse-tung, ideas in vogue during the late 1960s. In this vein Walker's grand statements of historical processes recall Luchino Visconti's *Il Gattopardo/The Leopard* (1963), in which Burt Lancaster plays an aging count who gives soliloquies on the decline of the aristocracy in 1860s Sicily.[19] However, the historical determinism communicated by the authors in *Burn!* is more convincing than that in *Kapò* and *The Battle of Algiers*, whose plots include unintended aspects, such as the unsettling narrative parallels between *Kapò* and the first Italian Holocaust drama, *L'ebreo errante/The Wandering Jew*, and the manner in which *The Battle of Algiers* seemingly rationalizes violence, given its subsequent appeal to both terrorist and counterterrorist groups. If *The Battle of Algiers* and *Kapò* have flaws in terms of their overreliance on ideological structures, *Burn!* is a film in which Pontecorvo reaches a higher cinematic level. *The Battle of Algiers* is a film about a successful revolution. But *Burn!* is about what happens before, during, and after revolution. *Burn!* is not limited by the historical scope of *The Battle of Algiers*, in which the action is reduced to the few years of the FLN uprising in Algiers. *Burn!* presents a more detailed account of the historical and cultural forces at work on the fictional Portuguese island. The story also examines a situation with continuing relevance—the exploitation of natural resources in an undeveloped country by a multinational company. Marlon Brando gives a brilliant interpretation of the Pygmalion-like relationship between the Englishman Walker and the ex-slave Josè Dolores, touching on the deeper issues of the paternalism, racism, and hypocrisy historically displayed toward third world peoples.

Despite the fact that he is directing a big-budget Hollywood production, Pontecorvo opens *Burn!* with the stylistic imprint of his earliest documentaries and first features. An opening shot of gulls flying over the sea recalls the first sequence of *The Wide Blue Road*. Pontecorvo replaces the anonymous narrator's summary of historical events from *The Battle of Algiers* with a short introduction by the captain of the English ship that brings Walker to the island of Queimada. The captain's commentary recalls the narrator's description of Squarcio's Mediterranean coastline in *The Wide Blue Road*, with a brief summary of the history of the island, which attained the name "Queimada" (burned) because in the 1520s the Portuguese decided to set the island ablaze in order to quell a revolt of the indigenous population they had enslaved. The film immediately confronts the topic of human slavery and the deep racial divide evident in the nineteenth century, when there was inadequate dialogue or recognition of the common humanity between Europeans and the non-European colonized peoples. The captain points out a rocky, bleached island in the bay whose white color is due to the skeletal remains of slaves who did not survive the voyage from Africa. The captain reports that the bodies of dead deportees were deposited by arriving slave ships before the ships moored in Queimada. In quick contrast to the bone-bleached island/mortuary, the captain presents the other side of Queimada, with its important commercial center, well-located port, bank, garrison, and the most famous bordello in the Antilles.

Like some Italian westerns, including those penned by Solinas in the late 1960s, the film focuses on two protagonists: an ascetic but often cruel Anglo figure and a more earthy Latin character.[20] Examples include the duality between Clint Eastwood and Gian Maria Volonte in Sergio Leone's westerns or the lazy trickster and gruff ogre duo in Bud Spenser and Terence Hills's *Trinity* series.

Renato Salvatori (Teddy Sanchez) left, Marlon Brandon (Sir William Walker) center, Evaristo Márquez (Josè Dolores) right, in Burn! *Courtesy of Photofest*

The recursion to such popular themes in the narrative eventually caused Pontecorvo to decline a credit as screenwriter.[21] In fact the final version of the screenplay is credited only to Giorgio Arlorio and Franco Solinas.

This dual-character narrative scheme from the Italian western would be important in the development in *Burn!* of the opposition between the English agent Sir William Walker and the water porter Josè Dolores, who, with Walker's help, becomes a Queimadan rebel leader. However, the choice to make such a clear narrative divide between the absolutely divergent backgrounds of the protagonists devalues the film's one mixed-heritage character, Teddy Sanchez, played by the veteran actor Renato Salvatori in blackface. Sanchez is Walker's contact when he first arrives on the island as a British agent hoping to foment a revolution against the Portuguese colonial government. Walker has a series of conversations with Sanchez, who indicates that despite his racial heritage, he feels white, a choice not surprising given his elevated position in Queimada society. Throughout the film Sanchez is portrayed as a weak and ineffectual figure who has the trust of neither the white commercial overlords nor the island's black, ex-slave population. The sense of an unbreachable barrier between the races and of the impossibility of dialogue is evident in this narrative devaluation of Teddy Sanchez. Walker dismisses Sanchez as a potential vehicle for the liberation struggles of the ex-slaves of Queimada, preferring Josè Dolores, a humble porter of pure African descent with whom the local population can identify more completely. The gentrified, multiracial Sanchez is, of course, compromised by his association with the moneyed interests of the island. But Sanchez is also presented as a figure who provokes the open disdain and disrespect of both protagonists, Walker and Dolores. The devaluation of the role of Sanchez seems like a search on the part of the authors for simplicity, so that the film is imbued with a narrative that emphasizes a Manichaeanist ethnic polarity.

In a key sequence Walker demonstrates to Teddy Sanchez the psychological difficulty of enslaved peoples in breaking free of subjugation. Walker tosses coins on the ground at the public square and then humiliates the locals, who fight among themselves to gather the money. The scene not only illustrates Walker's point about the ability of slavery to break the human spirit but also is an indirect humiliation of Sanchez, whom Walker has dismissed as too ineffectual and idealistic. Walker repeats the process of testing the willingness to accept humiliation with Josè Dolores, after seeing Dolores pick up a stone in anger toward a Portuguese soldier who has abused an enslaved woman holding her child. The freeze-frame of Josè's vindictive expression and the subjective camera reaction shot of the delight of Walker, who realizes he may have found a vehicle to remove the Portuguese from Queimada, repeats a sequence from *The Battle of Algiers* in which Ali Le Pointe is tripped by a

French youth while fleeing the police. It is not clear whether Pontecorvo used this freeze-frame technique because of his nonprofessional actors' difficulty in adequately reciting their roles, but the emblematic effects of the sequences are the same. Walker then tests Dolores further, trying to stir a violent reaction in him by accusing him of stealing Walker's bags and then calling his mother a whore. But, unlike the locals, who fought over Walker's coins and blindly follow his instructions, Josè Dolores passes the test by attacking Walker with a machete.

In later scenes Walker continues his attitude of commanding and haughty impatience with Sanchez in veiled repetitions of the scene in which he throws coins to porters and insults Josè Dolores's mother. Walker derides Sanchez, telling him that he is a worthless dreamer. Through repeated use of the island bordello as a setting, the authors also infer that the mother of Teddy Sanchez was like the whore insultingly used by Walker as a test of Josè Dolores's spirit. But, unlike Sanchez, Dolores proves his masculinity and viability as a vehicle for Walker's plans by not allowing Walker to insult his mother. Sanchez, on the other hand, is a weak character who hesitates before assassinating the Portuguese governor. Walker must hold Sanchez's arm and fire the shot for him. Sanchez subsequently makes a heroic declaration of independence over the agonizing body of the Portuguese governor, with Walker in the shadows guiding his actions.

The weakness of Sanchez extends to his cool relations with Josè Dolores, who feels that Sanchez is soiled by his association with the white elite. As a figure who is neither wholly Portuguese nor wholly African, Sanchez represents a potential indigenous identity for the island, but his characterization as a weakling and Walker's expositions on the inherently downtrodden and fatalistic attitude of the ex-slave population identify Sanchez as a puppet of the colonial/commercial interests rather than as a character who could potentially unify island factions. In fact during his brief term as Queimadan president Sanchez is duped by the postcolonial sugar conglomerate and deposed by Walker when he finally attempts to assert indigenous control over the island's sugar crop. Sanchez is a figure with vast resonance in postcolonial history, for his ineptitude leads to further civil strife and economic hardship for the islanders.

The revolutionary overthrow of the Portuguese government in *Burn!* takes place during carnival, a theme that Pontecorvo relied on heavily in *The Battle of Algiers*. Pontecorvo presents a masterful choreography of an African-influenced South American carnival. Through the carnival there is a role reversal between what is exalted and low. Before Teddy Sanchez, wearing an African mask, shoots the Portuguese governor, the governor relates to the English consul how African animist rituals have been absorbed by the Portuguese. The reduction of the Portuguese governor to a murdered corpse in the next sequence could be read as a carnival element. What is elevated is demeaned in a scene rich with irony, given his confident words about the stability of Portugal's cultural hold over the island moments prior to his own assassination.

In the next sequences the carnival process continues beyond the control of Walker and the Queimadan elite. The assassination of the Portuguese governor does not lead directly to the controlled constitutional process preferred by Teddy Sanchez and orchestrated by Walker, but leads to the unpredictable arrival of Josè Dolores and his army, who appear at the governor's residence like a temporary carnival king with a military retinue. When Walker reveals how he orchestrated events to the temporarily victorious Josè Dolores, the latter begins to understand the fleeting nature of his carnival-like transformation from slave porter to rebel general. Walker's lessons have developed only Josè's latent military skills, not his administrative ones. Walker poignantly asks Josè who will direct industry, teach in the schools, staff the hospitals, govern the island, and direct its commerce. When Walker points to Josè's men and warns him that at the moment they are not prepared to run the island infrastructure, he essentially repeats the scene when he threw coins to porters on the street and then demanded that the money be returned after they fought over it. The sequences are an effective allegory of the postcolonial experience, in which nominal control may be transferred to indigenous hands, but actual economic power remains in the hands of former colonial overlords. As the scene ends there is a montage depicting the disbanding of Josè Dolores's army as the prerevolutionary social order is reestablished after the carnival interlude.

Despite his recognition of the deep cultural and historical roots of carnival culture, as in his previous films, Pontecorvo ascribes a secondary role to religion in *Burn!* Walker organizes the first meeting of Josè Dolores's comrades in a church. But Walker's proposal to Josè Dolores and his comrades in the church is not about spiritual matters; it is about bank robbing. The choice of a place of religious worship as a venue to organize a crime again reveals the secondary importance the screenwriters and Pontecorvo ascribe to religious culture. Like the racially mixed Teddy Sanchez, religion is potentially a force for unity and cooperation, but it is devalued as merely another pretext for cultural domination. In the first sequences of the film Walker observes the garroting of Santiago, the rebel leader Walker had originally come to meet in Queimada at Teddy Sanchez's request. A prisoner informs Walker that the Portuguese will decapitate the lifeless corpse of Santiago as an affront to the animist beliefs of the local population, which feels that a body must be intact in death in order to remain complete in the afterlife. Thus the imposition of Christian faith on the population is just another aspect of Portuguese hegemony.

The second half of the film takes places ten years after Walker's initial orchestration of Queimadan independence from Portugal. The passage of time allows Pontecorvo to offer a documentary-like summary of events recounting the rise of the international sugar business. There is also a sequence in the London sugar exchange and a montage of the efforts of representatives of sugar companies to find Walker so he may help them quell a new revolt led by Josè Dolores in Queimada. But instead of the dashing, confident figure from the first half of the film, the sugar company agents find a drunken, brawling Walker estranged from his British wife, roaming the European coasts on a skiff called the *Adios* after being expelled from his club and having resigned his commission in the British navy. These scenes are supposed to indicate a loss of identity, of civilized status, for Walker, who is eager to return to Queimada as an employee of the Royal Sugar Company to regain the romantic spirit of adventure of his youth.

When Walker reappears in Queimada Pontecorvo affords himself an opportunity for a documentary montage of recent events, with Walker as his narrator, for an audience of the Queimadan elite. Events in Queimada in the ten years since Walker's departure are presented as exemplary of the process of exploitation by which multinational corporations, in this case a sugar conglomerate, impose their control on newly independent countries. Queimadan president Teddy Sanchez laments that its commercial agreements with the Royal Sugar Company have left the government of Queimada with no control over its own territory. The economic crisis faced by the newly independent Queimada government is supposed to echo the difficulties faced by ex-colonial governments dependent in international markets on the sale of their raw materials, in this case sugar.[22] The setting of Josè Dolores's revolt following riots on Queimada in the year 1848 is important in the context of European history as one of the years in which popular revolts changed the political map of Europe. In 1848 much of the continent rose up in popular revolt against the monarchist governments that had ruled the continent since the defeat of Napoleon's attempt at world conquest in the early nineteenth century.

During the course of the film, Walker gives the island elite several seminars. These seminars give the screenwriters a setting for an exposition of political and cultural ideas by authors like Frantz Fanon, which identify the colonial legacy as the origin of exploitation and social tensions in the third world. In his first speeches to the island elite in the first half of the film, Walker has to convince them to overthrow Portuguese rule. He offers a proto-Marxist analysis of the difference between a wife and a prostitute, with physical love as a product. The speech is supposed to impart the lesson of the larger historical context of the film—the shift from a traditional colonial structure to a neocolonial structure based on the exploitation of natural resources by commercial

*Marlon Brando (Sir William Walker) center, Thomas Lyons (General Prada)
second from right in* Burn! *Courtesy of Photofest*

agreement. In the traditional arrangement the colonial power has not only the benefits of profit but also the duty of ownership and governance. Walker proposes instead a strictly commercial model by which the profits from commerce are still available; but when neocolonial interests increase the slave's status to that of a wage earner, they are no longer subject to the duties of ownership. Thus for multinational corporations a prostitute (wage earner) is preferable to a wife (slave), and a free market system is preferable to the mercantile system of traditional colonialism. The parallel is a simplification that does not take into account a country's opportunities to create wealth by tapping into the creative initiative of its populace—or, to continue the prostitute parallel, the fact that marriage may be renegotiated or terminated through legal means.

When Walker returns to the island ten years later in the second half of the film, he continues his seminars and offers the commonplace about the manner in which ten years can reveal the contradictions of an entire century. But Walker's aphorism is rebutted by one of José's followers, Josino, whom Walker saves from a firing squad. Josino quotes José Dolores, saying that "it is better to know where to go without knowing how, than to know how to go but not know where. He adds that "a worker is a slave as along as there are bosses and those with land,"

and "therefore one should cut heads instead of cane." Finally, he declares, "If being civilized means being civilized according to white civilization it is better to be uncivilized." The simple and cruel message of Josè's violent manifesto pleases Walker, who romantically and paternalistically considers the vibrancy of Josè's worldview. As he sends Josino back to Josè Dolores with an invitation for a parley, Walker even asks a regular solider why he is not on the Sierra with Dolores.

At Walker's second seminar for the island elite after his return to the island, General Prada objects to Walker's characterization of Josè Dolores as a revolutionary figure, a legitimate vehicle for Queimadan political identity. The general, who was not privy to Josino's recitation of Josè Dolores's bloody political sayings, remarks that Josè Dolores is no Robespierre, the early leader of the French Revolution and the later reign of terror preceding the dictatorship of Napoleon. Robespierre's reign of terror was a precursor of later totalitarian state violence, whether carried out for class reasons or purportedly racial ones. The reference to Robespierre follows Josino's quotation of Josè Dolores that eventually it is better to cut heads than to come to terms with the Queimadan elite and the Royal Sugar Company. The film does not directly depict Josè Dolores as a figure who may install a Robespierre-like reign of terror. Dolores is instead presented as Walker's rebellious pawn and ultimately as his victim. Walker's absolute control over the destiny of Queimada is made clear when he orchestrates a coup to oust Teddy Sanchez from power. When Sanchez objects to Walker's methods, Sanchez offers bread to a crowd expelled from their mountain homes in order to deprive Josè Dolores of an indigenous support base. But Sanchez's offer to the desperate villagers results not in an expression of national unity but in a bread riot.

At his subsequent seminars to the general staff of the military, Walker recites another commonplace about guerilla fighters being better soldiers than paid conscripts. Walker informs the assembled table of the Queimada elite that the guerillas have only a life to lose, while a soldier risks livelihood, family savings, and lifestyle, a difference that makes the guerilla a powerful adversary. These considerations echo the strategy of guerilla leaders like China's Mao Tse-tung or the Vietnamese Ho Chi Minh. Brando would have a chance to repeat similar lines in his performance as Kurtz in *Apocalypse Now* (1979), Francis Ford Coppola's adaptation of Joseph Conrad's nineteenth-century English adventure novel, *Heart of Darkness.*

When Walker's army of English conscripts and the Queimadan army crush Josè Dolores's rebellion, the film offers scenes of the bombing and burning of villages and women and children fleeing their homes and burning forests. When the British consul complains about the destructiveness of Walker's methods, Pontecorvo uses the scene to allow Walker a speech about the domino theory, according to which the news of Dolores's success would spread to other islands. These images and this theory would have been familiar to 1969 audiences as Vietnam War references. But they there are also allusions to the techniques used by the British Empire in the Boer War (1899–1902). The English broke the revolt of the Dutch inhabitants by creating concentration camps to prevent the sympathetic populace from materially supporting the rebel fighters.

When Josè is captured it is finally his turn to lead a seminar, for the soldiers in Walker's army. As Josè passes evacuated villagers, they stand as if he were a head of state, and Pontecorvo's camera pans the faces of the evacuated villagers with a formalist style that recalls scenes from Aldo Vergano's *Outcry*. Once he is imprisoned in Walker's camp, Josè prophesies the inevitable end of white domination to a rapt audience of black Queimadan soldiers. Josè's statements are put into naturalistic language about island wildlife that recalls the naturalistic imagery used by Machiavelli in *The Prince* to describe political struggle.[23] When asked about his future, Josè explains that his mistrust of Walker and the island elite is so deep that he plans to seek death if they offer him life, for if they want him alive it must mean that that it serves their interests in some manner. Dolores's creed is that if freedom is something that can be given, it is not truly freedom.

Marlon Brando (Sir William Walker) riding center and Márquez (Josè Dolores) in Burn! *Courtesy of Photofest*

After Josè's seminar to the Queimada soldiers, Walker leads a final ban-
quet discussion with the victorious island elite regarding what to do with Josè.
Walker suggests they induce Dolores to betray his cause in order to avoid
turning him into a martyr. But when Walker eavesdrops on General Prada's
conversation with Josè, he hears Josè laugh at the general's offers. In the final
scenes between Dolores and Walker, Josè refuses Walker's offer of help to escape. Pontecorvo reportedly cut a great deal of dialogue from the final scenes
between Dolores and Walker and replaced it with sacred music.[24] It is not
clear whether this decision was dictated by Brando's increasing impatience
with Marquez's growing pains as an actor. The end result is that music is an
even more important part of *Burn!* than of Pontecorvo's previous films. For
example, Ennio Morricone's *Abolicao* theme, with the organ music, is a compromise between Pontecorvo's interest in classical sacred music and the sort
of sound track that Morricone had been writing for Cristaldi's spaghetti westerns. Another scene in which the film's score composer Ennio Morricone's
sound track mimics the tone of sacred music is the one in which Dolores's
army approaches the capital. The scene was originally to have been accompanied by the *Kyrie* from the *Missa Luba*, which combines epic/sacral and prim-
itive tones. But Morricone reportedly objected to the idea of mixing the
works of different composers in a film and composed a piece that Pontecorvo
liked even more and was eventually used in the film.[25]

A narrative innovation for Pontecorvo in *Burn!* is that Walker is not a direct paladin of traditional nationalism, like the French commander Mathieu or
the Algerian nationalists Ali Le Pointe and Kader in *The Battle of Algiers*.
When Walker returns to Queimada he works directly for the commercial interests of the Royal Sugar Company, and indirectly for the British Empire.
Walker laments the irony of his position as the person who raised Josè Dolores
to his position as rebel leader and who then must eliminate Dolores when he
rebels in the name of the very ideals about liberty and justice that had been
used to gain his trust. Ultimately, Walker is a hypocritical figure, since his identification with Josè Dolores is personal, rather than professional or ideological.
The classical Pygmalion tale of *Burn!* is arguably a story of unrequited love in
which a statue comes to life and then rejects its maker.

Burn! is an unjustly undervalued Pontecorvo feature film. Ultimately it is
a hybrid production: a film envisioned by a politically motivated Italian director with auteurist pretensions produced by an American studio interested in the
pecuniary return expected of Italian westerns in the late 1960s. The cuts made
to the film by the American studio are reminiscent of the fate of Vittorio De
Sica's *Stazione Termini/Indiscretion of an American Wife* (1953) starring Mont-
gomery Cliff, a film that was also a commercial and professional setback for its
makers. The value of *Burn!* is that the film does not suffer from the thematic

inconsistencies of *Kapò*, the rationalization of violence (both French and Algerian) in *The Battle of Algiers*, or the reliance on the rhetoric of collectivism that characterizes *The Wide Blue Road*. In *Burn!* Pontecorvo presents a parable about a historical transformation from traditional colonialism to postcolonialism in a manner that is extremely relevant to subsequent world history. Unlike Pontecorvo's previous films, the historical determinism of *Burn!* has remained relevant, even timeless. The film is one of the few major features to offer a valid interpretation of the cultural and political aftermath of slavery and the plight of postcolonial countries unable to break free of an economic cycle in which their sole means of sustenance is the exploitation of natural resources. The film also features a brilliant performance by Marlon Brando, whom Pontecorvo ably typecast as a vibrant physical figure confronted by a moral dilemma.

NOTES

1. *Un pugno di dollars/A Fistful of Dollars* (1964), *Per qualche dollaro in più/ For a Few Dollars More* (1965), *Il buono, il brutto, e il cattivo/The Good, the Bad, and the Ugly* (1966).

2. See Christopher Frayling, *Spaghetti Westerns: Cowboys and Europeans from Karl May to Sergio Leone* (London: I. B. Tauris, 1998).

3. Joan Mellen, *Filmguide to "The Battle of Algiers"* (Bloomington: Indiana University Press, 1973), 13.

4. Edward Said, "The Quest for Gillo Pontecorvo," *Interview* 18 no. 11 (November 1988): 90–93.

5. "Walker, William," *Microsoft Encarta Encyclopedia*, CD ROM, 1999.

6. Luigi Cipriani, M. Conciatori, M. Giraldi, and L. Ricci, eds., *Primo piano sull'autore Gillo Pontecorvo "La dittatura della verità"* (Rome: Designer, 1999), 32.

7. Irene Bignardi, *Memorie estorte a uno smemorato vita di Gillo Pontecorvo* (Milan: Feltrinelli, 1999).

8. Gillo Pontecorvo, "Intervista a Gillo Pontecorvo a cura di Tatti Sanguinetti," *Queimada!/Burn!* DVD (Rome: Eagle Pictures, 2003).

9. Pontecorvo, "Intervista."

10. Pontecorvo, "Intervista."

11. Pontecorvo, "Intervista."

12. Bignardi, *Memorie*.

13. Bignardi, *Memorie*, 154.

14. Bignardi, *Memorie*.

15. Bignardi, *Memorie*, 154.

16. Charlie Glass, "The Hour of the Birth of Death: Pontecorvo's Long Silence and the Demise of Political Film-making," *Times Literary Supplement*, June 28, 1998, 20.

17. Bignardi, *Memorie*, 153.

18. Bignardi, *Memorie.*

19. A. O. Scott, "Third World Revolution as a Product of Italian Design," *New York Times*, September 19, 2004.

20. Frayling, *Spaghetti Westerns.*

21. Bignardi, *Memorie.*

22. Paul Ryan, *Marlon Brando: A Portrait* (New York: Carrol and Graf, 1992), 138.

23. Josè Dolores's story of the falcon and falconer recalls Machiavelli's story of the fox and lion in chapter 17 of *The Prince*, "Whether It Is Better to Be Loved or Feared."

24. Said, "Quest," 90–93.

25. Bignardi, *Memorie.*

· 7 ·

The "Guilty Conscience" of *Ogro* (1979)

Gillo Pontecorvo. Courtesy of Photofest

*A*fter *Queimada!/Burn!* received a cool public and critical reception, Pontecorvo waited nearly ten years before releasing what would turn out to be his last feature film, *Ogro* (1979), an adaptation of the book *Operation Ogro: The Execution of Admiral Luis Carrero Blanco*, by Julen Agirre. Carrero Blanco, Spanish dictator Francisco Franco's (1892–1975) chosen successor, was blown

89

up by a bomb that Basque ETA terrorists had planted under the Madrid street where his car passed on December 20, 1973. On *Ogro* Pontecorvo would be working for the first time without his longtime writing partner, Franco Solinas. The screenplay of *Ogro* is credited to Giorgio Arlorio, Pontecorvo, and Ugo Pirro. Pontecorvo had reached a point of narrative consistency with *Burn!* in which the presentation of his ideas of historical determinism found a valid and convincing setting. However with *Ogro* he would be forced to face issues about the legitimacy of violence that had remained unresolved in his work since *La battaglia di Algeri/The Battle of Algiers*.

With *Ogro* Pontecorvo moved away from the action adventure genre of *Burn!* and back to the familiar territory of the *film politico* or instant movie. The term "instant movie" often refers to a current within Italian cinema of quickly produced films that exploit public interest in recent events. The economic constraints of these films actually recall the development of neorealism. Even Roberto Rossellini's neorealist masterpiece *Roma città aperta/Rome Open City* could be considered an instant movie, since it offers a version of events of the Nazi occupation of Rome from 1943 to 1944, with references to the *fosse Ardeatine* massacre.

Ogro was made during a period of retrenchment for the Italian film industry. In the summer of 1976 the Italian Corte Costituzionale, the highest court in the country, handed down a decision that opened the airwaves to private television stations. Instead of a monopoly of state television broadcasts from the RAI (Radio audiovisioni Italiane), the Italian public gained access to reruns of films and serials, such as older American productions. The new competition resulted in a drop in Italian cinema production in the 1970s. The television gap that had allowed the Italian film industry in the early 1960s to become the world's second-largest producer of films as Italians increasingly preferred television to a trip to the local theater.

Ogro has two historical backdrops. Firstly the film could be read as a thinly disguised examination of the Italian terrorist situation in the 1970s set in Basque Spain. In Italy the 1970s later became known as the *anni di piombo* (the years of lead), as the country experienced politically inspired terrorism from both extreme Left and Right. The left-wing terrorism from groups such as the Red Brigades was partly motivated by the course of the Italian Communist Party (PCI) at the time. In 1972 the PCI secretary Enrico Berlinguer sought a common ground with the ruling Christian Democrat (DC) coalition. Berlinguer's actions were in the spirit of postwar PCI secretary Palmiro Togliatti's pragmatic attempt to prevent splits in the Italian Left over disagreements about successive embarrassments regarding the Soviet Union. These included Khrushchev's so-called secret speech admitting Stalinist crimes and the suppression of popular revolts in Hungary in 1956 and

Czechoslovakia in 1968.¹ Pontecorvo was one of many who left the PCI following the Soviet Union's repression of prodemocracy demonstrations in Hungary in 1956. Berlinguer's adoption of a conciliatory attitude toward the ruling DC coalition became known as the *compromesso storico* (historic compromise), although it was arguably also a reaction to right-wing coups in Greece (1967), Chile (1973), and Portugal (1975) which made many in Italy's left wing, especially Berlinguer, fearful of a similar right-wing action in Italy following the electoral gains of the PCI in the early 1970s. DC leaders such as Moro sought to continue the policy of conquering and dividing the leftist opposition and thus received Berlinguer's overtures favorably. But the PCI's historic compromise with the DC alienated radical leftist factions. The PCI leadership found itself in the curious position of fearing a right-wing reaction if it abandoned its rapprochement with the DC and exacerbating left-wing terrorism if it remained cooperative with DC. Many of the PCI's supporters were suspicious of the new middle-class influences in the party, which had traditionally been proletarian. Given the political tensions, the Italian elections of the 1970s were some of the most hotly contested since 1948. The very narrow victory for the DC was aided considerably by the pro-Western wing of the Italian Socialist party (PSI), led by Bettino Craxi.²

The shadow over this entire period was the specter of political violence from both Right and Left. The starting point for the years of terrorism was the bombing at Piazza Fontana in Milan on December 12, 1969, which began a period not only of terrorist attacks but also of what became known as the "strategy of tension," during which violence—whether perpetrated by left-wing or right-wing terrorists—had the common goal of destabilizing republican institutions. Groups such as the communist Red Brigades were formed as a radical, activist version of leftist parties in the climate of the hedonistic youth movements of the early 1970s. But their members also included working-class youths who were raised with a memory of the resistance; some with apparently orthodox Catholic roots. The Red Brigades in particular saw their killing spree as a logical continuation of the resistance or the Italian equivalent of the Latin American left-wing insurgencies of the time. Eventually the violence of these Italian groups was directed against anyone identified with the status quo. The high point of Red Brigade action was the kidnapping of Christian Democrat leader Aldo Moro on March 16, 1978, and his murder on May 9, 1978.

Ogro was actually in production when the Moro kidnapping occurred. Pontecorvo's film was initially supposed to be a straight depiction of the assassination of Blanco by ETA commandos. But after events in Italy, Pontecorvo was forced to reconsider his own previously ideologically rigid stance on political violence, which was rooted in the resistance against Nazism/Fascism in

World War II. A film depicting the sort of violence in *The Battle of Algiers* might have been insensitive given events in Italy. Pontecorvo has subsequently stated that he completed *Ogro* with a guilty conscience.[3] The film was revised to include sequences portraying divisions within the ETA Basque movement after the death of Franco and the movement of Spain toward republican institutions. In particular Pontecorvo included a coda in which a majority of the Basque terrorists involved in the Carrero Blanco assassination seem to renounce violence at the hospital deathbed of their most hard-line comrade. Thus the film suffers from a thematic inconsistency, with sections that sympathetically portray the details leading to the assassination in contrast to flashforwards and flashbacks that question the legitimacy of violence.

In a film depicting the assassination of Carrero Blanco by an ETA Basque terrorist cell operating in Madrid, Pontecorvo also had to incorporate some understanding of the history of Basque subjugation to Castillian power, a topic much more complicated than the brief run-down that the documentary-like opening of the film allows. Most recognition of the ancient roots of Basque resistance to Castillian dominance dates back to the efforts to retain regional autonomy by the kingdom of Navarre in the fifteenth century.[4] The ETA terrorist movement is part of a millennial impulse for national liberation on the part of the Basque people, who have a linguistic and cultural identity unrelated to the dominant Castillian culture emanating from the capital city of Madrid.

There is a well-accepted identification of a Catholic origin to the Basque separatist movement, which is actually more defined than the nebulous connection between communist terrorists of the 1970s and their religious education in Italy. In fact a near majority of Basque terrorists in the 1960s and 1970s were apparently recruited from Catholic seminars and convents.[5] The first rumblings of contemporary Basque separatist violence against Castillian hegemony occurred in the early 1960s. During the same period Basque priests protested the church hierarchy, which they felt was too closely aligned with the Franco regime and devalued Basque language and cultural identity. In the film the Basque seminary teacher Joseba leaves his teaching post in order to join ETA. Joseba is a character who may be identified with the militancy of the Basque priesthood, which actively encouraged Basque nationalism. The name of the hard-line Basque terrorist in the film, Txabi, recalls one of the first Basque martyrs, Txabi Echevarrieta, who was gunned down by policemen in 1968, which in turn led to Basque retaliation with the murder of a high official in the Spanish police, Meliton Manzanas. The Spanish state reacted to the Manzanas murder by imposing a state of emergency in Basque regions and extending the use of torture and imprisonment without due process, gaining a reputation of handing out sentences on often scanty evidence. Some of those implicated in the Manzanas murder, including two priests, were put on trial in Burgos in 1970, an event that gained international press coverage and afforded ETA recognition as a vehicle for anti-Francoist resistance. Emboldened by the rise in popular support, ETA began policies of extortion and kidnappings and murders of policemen and police informants.[6]

In the years preceding the Carrero Blanco assassination, the regime of Dictator Francisco Franco was increasingly losing the support of the factions of Spanish society that had been its more solid supporters, such as the church and even the Spanish army. These changes in Spanish society during the declining years of the Franco dictatorship are fleetingly mentioned in the film, when the ETA commandos react to Spanish news broadcasts that refer to political events of 1970s Spain. The reality of the political situation in the early 1970s in Spain was that the physical decline of Franco mirrored the reduced resolve of his regime, to the point that the ETA assassination of Blanco accelerated the decline of the Falangist regime and indirectly fostered the path toward representative government in Spain. In the 1970s ETA ideology interpreted the Basque struggle for independence in the same terms as the efforts of colonized peoples to break free of foreign hegemony, a parallel that has never received much support among European governments, such as that of France, which also has Basque regions. The ETA activists of the 1970s also apparently regarded the Algerian achievement of independence from France in the 1950s as a model for their own national liberation struggle. This may be a reason why Pontecorvo was attracted to the subject. The theme of national liberation imbued with socialist political teachings seemed to make the Basque situation ideal for a filmmaker like Pontecorvo, who enjoyed stories with echoes of the Italian anti-Nazism/Fascism resistance struggle during World War II. The problem with the Algerian model for ETA was that much of the wealth in the Basque regions is reportedly in Basque hands, and even in the 1970s some of the working classes were actually comprised of non-Basques attracted to the region by opportunities for employment.[7] Thus the class element in the Algerian struggle—with Algerians economically subjugated to the wealthier French colonials—was not a parallel for the Basque setting.[8]

Like many of Pontecorvo's films, *Ogro* opens as if it were a documentary, with scenes from Spanish history of the 1970s, including cameos of aging Spanish dictator Francisco Franco and his chosen successor, Carrero Blanco. Pontecorvo also includes images indicating the movement in Spain after Franco's funeral away from Falangist dictatorship toward republican institutions. These images are accompanied by a voice-over that briefly details the origins of the ETA Basque struggle for national autonomy and the persecutions Basques have suffered under the Franco regime. There is even a map of the Basque province within Spain, which, however, excludes Basque regions in France.

After the documentary opening, *Ogro* adopts a narrative strategy of flashbacks and flash-forwards that recalls the structure of *The Battle of Algiers*, which begins with scenes of French forces surrounding the hideout of Ali Le Pointe and then fades back to detail the rise of Ali as a leader of the FLN Algerian independence movement. *The Battle of Algiers*, in effect, has two endings. In one the French counterinsurgents are able to quash the FLN rebellion in the Casbah of Algiers, and in the other a popular revolt is accompanied by a voice-over that indicates the eventual achievement of independence from France. *Ogro*, like *The Battle of Algiers*, has a narrative structure of flashbacks and flash-forwards as well as two endings, but the story line is reversed. The main content of the film, the details of the Blanco assassination, is a story of an insurgent victory, since the ETA terrorists successfully carried out their scheme and murdered Franco's vice president. But instead of the popular uprising coda in *The Battle of Algiers*, *Ogro* ends with a hospital deathbed scene in which the majority of the ETA commandos who orchestrated the Blanco assassination seem to renounce violence. Thus the terrorist violence is framed by a coda that does not lead to independence, as in *The Battle of Algiers*. Rather the deathbed scenes with the hard-line Txabi point to the possibility of a shift in Basque strategy to work within the republican institutions of post-Franco Spain.

The film opens in Bilbao (Euszkadi), the capital of the Basque region of Spain in 1978, as the ETA terrorist Txabi is walking along the city dockyards, stalked by his estranged wife, Amayore. The flashbacks and flash-forwards centering on Txabi and Amayore's troubled marriage attempt to enhance the human qualities of the terrorists. In interviews Pontecorvo has confirmed that these flash-forward and flashbacks gained importance after the Moro kidnapping and murder made Pontecorvo and his producers wary of the public reception of a film that was a straight documentation of a terrorist operation.[9] The attempt to enhance a narrative through a love story had already been tried with mixed results in *Kapò*, and are no more convincing in *Ogro*. Txabi and Amayore hold a heated discussion about political activism and ideology in which Amayore presents the arguments of the Basque factions that would like to work within the context of a post-Franco Spain. Despite Amayore's pleas, Txabi remains a hard-line believer in armed struggle and terrorism, more interested in attaining an absolute change in people's consciousness than a tangible political victory.

The film concludes with a return to these opening scenes in 1978 Euszkadi between Txabi and Amayore, five years after the depiction of Blanco's assassination, which forms the central section of the film. Txabi leaves Amayore in order to murder two Guardia Civil policemen by shooting them in the back. One of the fallen officers returns fire, mortally wounding Txabi. The last sequences of the film depict Txabi agonizing on his hospital deathbed. Before entering the room where Txabi lays in agony, a reporter briefly interviews Txabi's superior in the Blanco operation, Esarra, who gives the reporter a short statement about the inappropriateness of armed struggle in post-Fascist Spain. Esarra, like Amayore, hopes that 1978 Spain is on the road to democracy after the death of dictator Francisco Franco. Unlike the hard-line Txabi, Esarra is a member of the Basque independence movement who has chosen to work within the system. In the hospital room there is a discussion between the dying Txabi and Esarra about the legitimacy of armed struggle and violence. Txabi repeats the gist of his earlier statements to Amayore— that it takes an inhuman patience to accept the injustice of the world and work within the world to change it. Yet he also admits that he fears death and final judgment, a brief acknowledgment of the religious background of many of the ETA activists. Esarra responds that the courage of men like Txabi is also needed, as the film ends. In interviews Pontecorvo has emphasized the importance of Esarra's admission to the agonizing Txabi that his kind of "courage is necessary," as a rationalization for the intransigent position of the impenitent terrorist.[10]

With the characterization of Txabi and Esarra as representatives of two opposing political views, the film harks back to the stiff ideological divisions between characters in Pontecorvo's earlier films like *La grande strada azzurra/The Wide Blue Road* and *Kapò*. In *Ogro* the Basque terrorists are divided between the true believers, represented by Txabi, and moderates, represented by Esarra, who are willing to attenuate violence, so that the post-Franco regime in Spain may start the process of democratization of the country's institutions. By giving the film's final words to the more moderate Esarra, Pontecorvo redresses the direction taken in *Burn!* in which a Teddy Sanchez, is depicted as an ineffectual puppet. In fact, *Ogro* is the only Pontecorvo film in which seemingly moderate characters are allowed significant room in the plot. Pontecorvo has stated that an aim of the film was to portray Txabi as someone who "was not a monster," and was instead driven by an uncompromising desire to remake man and society.[11] But unlike the coda of *The Battle of Algiers*, which celebrates a popular revolt, the coda of *Ogro* has an opposite effect. Txabi comes across as precisely the sort of hard-line monster who devalues human life and is capable of rationalizing violence in the name of an ideological goal nebulously mired in anarchist political jargon about the revolutionary recreation of human consciousness. In *Burn!* General Prada points out that Josè Dolores may not have been a Robespierre for the simple reason that he was unable to retain power. But Txabi in *Ogro* seems to be a figure capable of finding a political or ideological rationalization for the most extreme violence.

One of the narrative flaws in Pontecorvo's earlier films is the lack of attention given to religion. Unlike in Pontecorvo's other films, in *Ogro* religion and religious imagery play a key role, which reflects the historical influence of the Basque priesthood on the rise of the ETA in the 1960s and 1970s. After the initial scenes between Txabi and Amayore, there is a flashback to the boyhood of the future terrorist commandos in a Spanish school in which a teacher upbraids them and smacks their hands for speaking Basque in school. In retaliation the boys go out at night to spray paint pro-ETA slogans on the walls of the city streets until they are spotted and chased by the police. In the next scene Joseba, a priest teaching in the school, informs the entire class that he will give up his tranquil life as a priest in order to join the ETA resistance. Pontecorvo offers a zoom into the face of Txabi as a boy as Joseba explains his decision to commit his life to Basque nationalism. The same shot is used in *The Battle of Algiers* and in *Burn!* to indicate the moment in which a character gains a sense of political mission.

The idea of a nexus between communist terrorism and Catholic upbringing, the so-called Catto-Communist connection, explains the recurring religious references made by Txabi. In *Ogro* Joseba, the ex-priest turned terrorist who is Txabi's mentor, reappears leading the February 1973 vote of an ETA terrorist council to decide whether to kidnap Carrero Blanco and ask for an exchange of 150 political prisoners, or to simply assassinate him. The majority vote in favor of kidnapping. But Txabi votes with the losing minority, opting for assassination. After the vote, Joseba chides Txabi for having retained an orthodox mentality like a priest because of the ideological rigidity demonstrated by his inability to accept a compromise—the choice to kidnap Blanco in hopes of an exchange for imprisoned ETA activists. Instead Txabi opts for a more brutal course of action—the assassination of Blanco. In the 1978 scenes between Txabi and Amayore, set in Bilbao five years after the Blanco assassination, Txabi is the only member of the Blanco assassination team who remains a terrorist. Txabi explains his break with his former comrades to Amayore in biblical terms, as a betrayal between brothers. Txabi's deathbed rationalization of terrorist violence is replete with references to God and a final judgment. Pontecorvo's staging of Txabi's agony on his deathbed has elements of religious imagery and is accompanied by an Ennio Morricone sound track of sacred organ music. Pontecorvo allows Txabi—like Ali Le Pointe in *The Battle of Algiers*—a quasi-religious representation as a figure who expires as a martyr for a national liberation struggle. Yet Txabi is ultimately not a heroic figure. His rigidity clashes with the pragmatic, life-affirming decisions of his former comrades, who have seemingly renounced violence.

While in *The Battle of Algiers* French atrocities rationalize Algerian terrorism and Algerian atrocities rationalize French suppression, in *Ogro* the only setting in which Carrero Blanco appears is in a church. Blanco's daily routine of attending mass in a humble Madrid chapel originally inspired ETA plans to kidnap him, according to the accounts in Agirre's book. In these church scenes a subjective camera from the point of view of Esarra pans over the faces of worshippers as the other Basque commandos attempt to identify which of the congregation are Blanco's bodyguards. The film does make some effort to equate the political power of the Franco regime with the historic collusion of the Catholic Church. When Blanco is given a promotion in Franco's regime, the film portrays Blanco receiving congratulations in the same Madrid chapel. But the day of the bombing includes an extended sequence from Blanco's daily mass and the segment of the rites in which the presiding priest offers parishioners forgiveness for their sins. In these sequences there are repeated close shots of Blanco accepting the host during communion. Pontecorvo relies heavily on Ennio Morricone's musical soundtrack accompanying the priest distributing the host, with subjective shots of the Basque terrorist Icar watching Blanco take communion. Blanco's only line in the film is when he says, "Amen" and accepts the host after the priest recites the ritual formula "body of Christ." Rather than making a convincing political statement about the collusion between the Francoist state and the church, the scenes recall Shakespeare's *Hamlet* (act 3, scene 3), in which the Danish prince hesitates before killing his uncle, who is kneeling in prayer. Agirre's book relates that the Basque commandos referred to Blanco by the code name "Ogre." But none of the causes for this visceral antagonism are evident in these brief sequences. The only depictions of Blanco highlight his religious practices and do not adequately connect him with the political issues that led the Basques to target him for assassination. That the Ogre, Blanco, appears only as a figure saying "Amen" and receiving communion does not help the film portray the Basque commandos in a sympathetic light. Besides these appearances in religious settings and brief historical newsreel footage with Franco, Blanco is an almost anonymous figure.

One of the great strengths of the Italian neorealist style that so heavily influenced Pontecorvo was an objective portrayal of reality that offered the mentality and motivation of both the protagonists and the antagonists in a story. However, the film attempts to create narrative tension by focusing on disagreements between the hard-line Txabi and his more moderate comrades, which culminate with their discussion about the legitimacy of violence at Txabi's hospital deathbed. The terrorists' arguments about whether to kill or kidnap Blanco that begin the film and the November 23, 1973, ETA executive vote to assassinate Blanco after the killing of Joseba are supposed to have a wider political context. Those in favor of kidnapping, like Esarra, are later willing to work with the new Spanish government. Those, like Txabi, in favor of assassination remain fixed in their adhesion to the idea of violent armed struggle. These divisions are still heated topics in the Basque independence movement. The difficulty with this plot strategy is that all of these characters are on the same political side. In the film the figures who represent Castillian oppression of Basque self-determination are the school teacher who punishes the future terrorists for speaking Basque and, more importantly, Blanco, as a part of Franco's regime. Instead of offering a direct characterization of Blanco as a Castillian oppressor of Basque identity, the film repeats themes of collectivism versus individualism from *Kapò*, with a concentration on the mindset of hard-line Txabi. The Basque terrorist's failed marriage with Amayore, the influence he gains from the priest turned terrorist Joseba, and his deathbed debate with Esarra form a framework that contains the action of the film.

Despite the opening in the religious classroom depicting the suppression of the Basque language and the creation of a connection between Joseba and the commandos, Pontecorvo's film communicates little sense of Basque identity. There is a brief scene indicating popular Basque support for the ETA in Bilbao, as ships sound their sirens and Guardia Civil policemen tear down posters announcing the death of Joseba. In Madrid Esarra has a chance encounter with a little Basque girl who recognizes him as Basque. But these attempts to give the commandos some hint of humanity are unsuccessful. Agirre's book includes anecdotes about the terrorists going to a party in Madrid frequented by Basques and being immediately identified as activists by their countrymen and about Madrileños joking that anyone with a Basque accent must be in the ETA. These stories are much less dry and forced than the attempt at the humanization of the terrorists via Txabi and Amayore's marital troubles in *Ogro*. The film does not capitalize on the details supplied in the book by Agirre, with its rich anecdotes about the difficulties of the Basque terrorists' operation and their collegial attitude. Even though Pontecorvo has claimed he met with ETA activists in preparation for the film, it does not adequately communicate the cultural estrangement the Basques felt in the capitol city, Madrid.

The segments that comprise the bulk of the film—the claustrophobic and suffocating re-creation of the clandestine life of the Basque commandos in Madrid and the minute details of their preparation for the Blanco car bombing—are presented as sidebars to episodes of Txabi's strict adherence to liberation ideology. Ennio Morricone's heroic drum and fife motif does little to increase the dramatic tension of these sequences, which create little empathy for the Basques. In one sequence Txabi laments the lack of interest in fighting Franco and the Fascists among the Madrileños. He observes a bus-load of Real Madrid soccer team supporters and tells his comrades how alien-ated he feels from the inhabitants of the capitol—a rare anecdote from the book. In an extended sequence Txabi listens to the police radio, against the orders of Esarra, and he learns that the Guardia Civil is suppressing a strike. Txabi heroically saves a union organizer from arrest and subsequently sug-gests to Esarra that they contract this labor organizer to build a wall needed to soundproof a basement where they plan to hold the kidnapped Blanco. Tx-abi's encounter with the union organizer is replete with the rhetoric of worker solidarity, Gramscian consciousness, and collective action, which recalls scenes from *The Wide Blue Road* and *Kapò*. But there is little in these scenes that communicates Txabi's sense of Basque identity. The result is that Txabi's mindset comes across as a confusing mixture of Bakunite insurrectionalism and Catholic irrationalism.

Unlike in Pontecorvo's earlier films, there is little sense of carnival mas-querade or contrast between high and low in *Ogro*. Pontecorvo's previous films rely on an inversion of roles from most abject to most powerful. In *Kapò* the frightened deportee Edith becomes the feared kapò Nicole. In *Burn!* Teddy Sanchez dons an African carnival mask and shoots the Portuguese governor during carnival with Walker's help. Josè Dolores is transformed from bag-carrying slave to nationalist rebel general. In *The Battle of Algiers* Alger-ian women dress as Westerners in order to plant bombs among the French. The arrogant French commander Colonel Mathieu is eventually defeated by Ali Le Pointe, the lowly ex-ruffian turned FLN militant. But in *Ogro* the masquerades are not as convincing. One of the ETA band impersonates a sculptor in order to rent a basement studio where the commandos will dig the tunnel to blow up Carrero Blanco. But the presentation of the steps leading to the bombing and the characterization of Joseba and Txabi as former priests turned terrorists does not communicate the sense of liberating carnival-like reversals of Pontecorvo's other films. The purported ogre and villain of the story, Carrero Blanco, is a penitent churchgoer instead of a forbidding figure of unforgiving power and violence.

When the film was released Italian critics were actually quite generous. Some critics accurately perceived that the film is a thinly veiled recreation of the situation in 1978 Italy within a framework that echoes the identification of a Catholic-communist undercurrent in the Italian Red Brigades.[12] How-ever, given the context of events in Italy after the Aldo Moro kidnapping and murder, the flashbacks and flash-forwards that attempt to put the question of armed struggle and terrorism into some sort of context are ultimately uncon-vincing. Instead of enhancing the genre of Italian political cinema—films with rich political backdrops like Francesco Rosi's *Il caso Mattei/The Mattei*

Affair (1972) or *Salvatore Giuliano* (1962)—*Ogro* has the staged predictability of Hollywood films about Allied actions behind enemy lines during World War II, without adequate characterizations to rationalize the use of violence. Pontecorvo has stated that he was attracted to the subject because of his days in the resistance. However, the film is a claustrophobic adaptation of the source material by Agirre in which the sense of paranoia outweighs any sense of victory at the result of the terrorists' actions. Despite the services of an actor of the caliber of Gian Maria Volontè (as Esarra), none of the characters come across as sympathetic, and the film actually reduces empathy for the Basque cause.

Pontecorvo himself has admitted to having no great love for the final product of *Ogro*.[13] But the roots of the inconsistencies in *Ogro* are actually evident in Pontecorvo's previous features. *Ogro* has the heavy-handed ideological characterizations of *The Wide Blue Road* and *Kapò*. The film also suffers from a tendency to rationalize violence evident in *The Battle of Algiers*. *Ogro* does attempt to arrive at an anticipation of historical currents—as in *Burn!*—by depicting the split in the Basque independence movement. But *Ogro's* placement in Pontecorvo's career as a swan song gives it an added importance in the consideration of his overall work. With the codas and flashbacks that contradict the theme of the main section of the film, portraying the Blanco assassination, Pontecorvo attenuates his earlier ideological certainty about the legitimacy of armed struggle. The depth of this ideological retreat would become even graver in the few documentaries and shorts that Pontecorvo completed after *Ogro*, such as *Ritorno ad Algeri/Return to Algiers* (1992) and *Nostalgia di protezione/Protection Nostalgia* (1997).

NOTES

1. Berlinguer published a series of articles in *Rinascita*, October 5 and 9, 1973, entitled *Riflessioni Sull'Italia dopo i fatti di Cile*, which have been defined as the beginning of the *Compromesso storico* for their invitation to seek common ground with the DC and prevent a further slide toward authoritarianism by the liberal pro-American parties.

2. Marga Cottino-Jones, *A Student's Guide to Italian Cinema*, 2nd ed. (Dubuque, IA: Kendall Hunt, 1992).

3. Irene Bignardi, *Memorie estorte a uno smemorato vita di Gillo Pontecorvo* (Milan: Feltrinelli, 1999), 162.

4. See Marianne Heiberg, *The Making of the Basque Nation* (New York: Cambridge University Press, 1989), 103.

5. Heiberg, *Making*, 103.

6. Heiberg, *Making*, 106–7.

7. Heiberg, *Making*, 112–13.

8. Heiberg, *Making*.

9. Gillo Pontecorvo, "Intervista a Gillo Pontecorvo," *Ogro*, DVD (Rome: Cristaldi Film, 2003).

10. Corinne Lucas, "Political Terrorism in *Ogro*: An Interview with Gillo Pontecorvo," in *The Cineaste: Interviews on the Art and Politics of the Cinema*, ed. Dan Georgakas and Lenny Rubenstein (Chicago: Lake View, 1983), 307–12.

11. Lucas, "Political Terrorism," 3.

12. Callisto Cosulich, *Ogro*, *Paese sera*, November 10, 1979. Francesco Bolzoni, *Ogro*, *Avvenire*, September 5, 1979, sees the film as a remake of John Huston's *We Were Strangers* (1949); "Contenuti extra," *Ogro*, DVD (Rome: Cristaldi Film, 2003).

13. Luigi Cipriani, M. Conciatori, M. Giraldi, and L. Ricci, eds., *Primo piano sull'autore Gillo Pontecorvo "La dittatura della verità"* (Rome: Designer, 1999), 34.

· 8 ·

Pontecorvo's Retreat:
Ritorno ad Algeri/Return to Algiers (1992) and *Nostalgia di protezione/ Protection Nostalgia* (1997)

A QUARTER CENTURY OF FALSE STARTS

Ogro (1979) turned out to be Pontecorvo's last feature film. However, before the beginning of his retirement from feature filmmaking Pontecorvo showed interest in a number of projects. The type of film he rejected and the repetition of his reasons for refusing reveal much about his inability to commit to something about which he was not absolutely convinced. Some of the projects Pontecorvo refused in the early 1960s later became important films, although without the sort of lasting relevance of *La battaglia di Algeri/The Battle of Algiers*. For example, Pontecorvo was approached about directing a film version of a Pier Paolo Pasolini's work, which Pasolini eventually directed himself as *Accattone/The Scrounger* (1962), a film of undoubted social significance but without issues with the direct political immediacy to retain Pontecorvo's interest. Pontecorvo was also approached to work on *Io la conoscevo bene/I Knew Her Well* (1965), written by Scola and Maccari and eventually directed by Antonio Pietrangeli. *Io la conoscevo bene* is the story of an indolent young woman who leaves her hometown near Pistoia, in Tuscany, for Rome. She works a series of jobs—as housekeeper, hairdresser, usherette, cashier— has a series of squalid affairs, and eventually enters show business working in commercials and as an extra. When she becomes pregnant, she has an abortion and commits suicide by jumping out of a window. Again, as with the Pasolini project, such a microcosmic story lacked the sense of wider political urgency of Pontecorvo's features like *The Battle of Algiers* and *Queimada!/Burn!*[1]

Pontecorvo also reportedly contributed, with his writing partner Franco Solinas, to the script of *Le soldatesse/The Camp Followers* (1965), a novel by Ugo Pirro eventually directed by Franco Zurlini. Pirro's stories have also been

103

the subject of important films such as *Indagine su un cittadino al di sopra ogni sospetto/Investigation of a Citizen above Suspicion* (1970), *A ciascuno il suo/We Still Kill the Old Way* (1967), *Il giardino dei Finzi Continis/The Garden of the Finzi Continis* (1970), *La classe operaia va in paradiso/The Working Class Goes to Heaven* (1971), and *Metello* (1970), all landmarks in the genre of political cinema, or *cinema impegnato*. Explanations from Pontecorvo biographer Irene Bignardi and other sources regarding his withdrawal from these projects vary. For example, Pontecorvo apparently withdrew from *The Camp Followers* because the producer protested that Pontecorvo's treatment eliminated all of the action sequences, thus compromising the film's commercial appeal.[2] The book and the later film by Zurlini tell the story of a young Italian army officer in 1942 in Greece charged with the transport of fifteen prostitutes who are to service Italian soldiers. Pirro had tried to make a film of the story as early as 1950. His dedication to the project led to a film, now considered a minor classic, that was released in 1965 and subsequently hauled before Italian courts, charged with defamation of the military forces.

Before he finally decided to make *Burn!* Pontecorvo's search for potentially acceptable projects led him to experiment in paranormal phenomenon. He worked with Fausta Leoni on a series of four television programs on the paranormal, magic, and near-death experiences. The research for *Karma* gave Pontecorvo the opportunity to travel widely in order to search out stories about magic in years in which he also allegedly participated in an LSD experiment.[3]

In the early 1970s Pontecorvo's name appeared in connection with a film to be entitled *Confino Fiat* about a section of the Fiat factory in Turin where the workers most active in labor unions were separated from their colleagues. A film on the subject was eventually made by Ettore Scola, *Trevico-Torino: Viaggio nel Fiat-Nam/Trevico-Turin: Voyage in Fiat-Nam* (1973). In it, a young southern Italian immigrant moves to Turin, where he works as an assembly line worker for Fiat; the film features an effective combination of narrative and documentary sequences.

Other projects were brought to Pontecorvo. Producer Franco Cristaldi was interested in making a film out of *The Moskat Family*, a novel by Isaac Bashevis Singer that depicts the lives of Jews in Warsaw from 1911 to the late 1930s. The novel recounts the tragic events surrounding protagonists facing obliteration by the Nazis. The story had a particular relevance to Pontecorvo because of the diaspora of his own family after the passing of the *leggi raziali* in 1938. In fact many of Pontecorvo's brothers and sisters ended up living and working outside of Italy, and his parents narrowly escaped deportation by fleeing to Switzerland in 1943.

The most enigmatic of Pontecorvo's false starts back in the early 1970s was a film about Jesus Christ. American producers in particular were excited about the possibility of a Pontecorvo version of the life of Jesus to be entitled *Il tempo della fine/The Time of the End*, which would echo the plot line of *The Battle of Algiers* with Jesus as a reluctant Messiah leading a protest movement against the occupying Roman army. But the film never reached production. The studios producing the film insisted on a name actor to play Christ, and Pontecorvo refused, hoping to be able to continue in the neorealist style of casting nonprofessional actors, as he had done in *The Battle of Algiers* and *Burn!*[4] On the surface the film seems to have an inherent contradiction between the topic of violence within the context of national liberation, in this case the struggle of the Jews for liberation from imperial Rome, and Christ's ethical code, which unequivocally rejects violence and worldly aspirations.

Pontecorvo was approached by Donald Sutherland to direct a biopic on Norman Bethune based on the biography *The Scalpel, the Sword* by Ted Allen and Sydney Gordon. Bethune (1890–1939) was a Canadian surgeon active in international medical and humanitarian missions. He also served as a doctor in World War I and the Spanish Civil War, was wounded several times, and was by all accounts a committed left-wing activist. He was particularly well regarded by the Maoist regime in China, which made him into a national hero because he died of blood poisoning in 1939 in China due to a lack of medical supplies. The film *Bethune: The Making of a Hero* (1990) was eventually made without Pontecorvo, with Sutherland in the leading role.[5]

Despite their legendary arguments on the set of *Burn!* Marlon Brando proposed Pontecorvo as director of a Columbia Pictures film about the Battle of Wounded Knee and American Indian issues to be written by noted screenwriter Abby Mann. After overcoming his initial surprise about being recommended by Brando, Pontecorvo went to South Dakota, where he lived briefly with an Indian family on the Pine Ridge Reservation to conduct research. The producers withdrew and the project was abandoned after Brando promised an Indian rights organization final approval on the script.[6]

One film on which Pontecorvo worked with his longtime collaborator Solinas that almost came to fruition was *Monsieur Klein/Mr. Klein* (1976). The script, which Pontecorvo and Solinas wrote, was later filmed by Joseph Losey without significant modifications.[7] Pontecorvo dropped out once French actor Alain Delon became the producer and announced his intention to play the starring role. Pontecorvo was unwilling to compromise his ideas about the importance of having nonprofessional actors, harkening back to the heroic days of neorealism and films such as Vergano's *Il sole sorge ancora/Outcry* and Rossellini's *Paisan/Paisà*.

Of all of Pontecorvo's numerous unfinished projects *Mr. Klein* contains many of the features of a Pontecorvo-Solinas collaboration. The film's opening scene depicts the humiliation of a racial physical exam, a historical occurrence during the period of Nazi rule in Europe. People who feared deportation would submit themselves to a medical examination in order to receive a certificate proving their Aryan physiognomy and increase their chances of avoiding deportation. The film then shifts to a scene in which a Jewish man, desperate for money and expecting deportation, sells a painting to the art dealer Klein, played brilliantly by Delon despite Pontecorvo's apprehensions, a character who has enriched himself on the misfortune of those who must sell in the face of the Vichy-Nazi pogroms. The film concentrates on the duality between Klein, the venal and opportunistic art dealer, and another never seen and mysterious figure who assumes Klein's identity. With this duality the film's script repeats narrative strategies from Pontecorvo and Solinas's other collaborations. Like *Kapò, The Battle of Algiers*, and *Burn!* the film develops two characters who present opposing social, economic, and racial realities. Exposure to the difficulties of his unfortunate double has a monumental effect on the mindset of Klein, whose name and identity have been appropriated. The technique of using two opposite characters to provoke the privileged character into understanding the mindset of the other is a commonplace in Italian westerns, including those penned by Solinas in the 1960s.[8] In *Mr. Klein*, as in their other films, Pontecorvo and Solinas were interested in the process by which assumptions about life and one's role in society may be questioned after a change in social status. The themes and narrative course in *Mr. Klein* are actually similar to that of *Kapò*, in which an innocent Parisian schoolgirl Edith is transformed into Nicole, a cruel kapò in a Nazi work camp. Both films feature protagonists who reject their former identity. Like *Kapò*, *Mr. Klein* concludes with an act of self-sacrifice after the protagonist has attained a sense of awareness about his role in the oppression of others. In the film's final scenes Mr. Klein allows his own destruction by going to the infamous Velodrome roundup of Parisian Jews in the place of his double, a finale that recalls *Kapò*, in which Edith allows herself to be killed so the other prisoner may escape. Like *Kapò*, *Mr. Klein* has narrative elements recalling the unsettling themes of Alessandrini's *L'ebreo errante/The Wandering Jew*. When the film opens the gentile Mr. Klein, played by Alain Delon, is opportunistically buying artwork from Jews desperate for money during the pogroms in Vichy France. By taking advantage of these desperate people, Klein is acting with the venality and self-serving attitude that are historic planks of anti-Jewish propaganda. When Klein realizes that someone has assumed his identity, he takes steps to protect himself. His effort to prove his Aryan identity through genealogical research reveals that one of his grandparents was Jewish, living in Algeria. In the deportation sequence at the Paris Velodrome Klein's friend brings documentation attesting to Klein's Aryan status that could reverse his deportation orders. In the final sequence Klein ignores his friend and willingly enters the train destined for a Nazi extermination camp.

One project that Pontecorvo came quite near to completing was a film about the assassinated archbishop of El Salvador, Oscar Romero, whose death gained worldwide attention and brought the ideas of liberation theology to the forefront of public consciousness. On the surface the topic seemed made to order for Pontecorvo. In the late 1970s the Central American country of El Salvador was in a state of civil war, with an oligarchy of the heirs of the Spanish Empire fighting against a guerilla movement supported by Cuba and the Soviet Union. The story of popular struggle recalled moments in Pontecorvo's filmography as well as his past as a resistance fighter in World War II. Of course the film's protagonist was to be a Catholic prelate, an interesting figure given the limited references to organized religion in Pontecorvo's completed films. Unfortunately for Pontecorvo, an American production was already underway, which resulted in the film *Romero* (1989) directed by John Duigan, starring Raul Julia.[9]

Other potential Pontecorvo projects included a proposal that he complete Sergio Leone's unfinished film project on the siege of Leningrad. He was also approached to direct a film about an airplane crash in the Andean Mountain eventually done as *Alive* (1992). He was asked to consider doing a film version of *Il peccato/The Sin*, a book by Pasquale Festa Campanile (1980) about a priest and a sickly girl, set in World War I.[10] Many of Campanile's scripts had been made into important films, such as *Rocco e i suoi fratelli/Rocco and His Brothers* (1960) and *Il Gattopardo/The Leopard* (1963), by Luchino Visconti, and *Le quattro giornate di Napoli/The Four Days of Naples* (1962), by Nanni Loy. *Il peccato* was reportedly offered to Pontecorvo by producer Dino De Laurentis and would have offered Pontecorvo an opportunity to join forces with a screenwriter, Campanile, of the caliber of Franco Solinas, Pontecorvo's writing partner until *Ogro*.[11]

Despite the immense prestige and influence he enjoyed as a filmmaker, Gillo Pontecorvo made very few films. It is ironic that during the late 1970s and 1980s, when so many films with highly charged political themes were being made, Pontecorvo was unable to complete a feature film besides *Ogro*. Political films of this period include Giuseppe Ferrara's *Cento giorni a Palermo/One Hundred Days in Palermo* (1984), Richard Attenborough's *Gandhi* (1982), Oliver Stone's *Salvador* (1986), Roland Joffé's *The Killing Fields* (1984), Peter Weir's *The Year of Living Dangerously* (1982), and Roger Spottiswoode's *Under Fire* (1983). In interviews Pontecorvo has defended himself by explaining that he had trouble involving himself completely in a project unless it could consume him and convince him that it had to be made. If Pontecorvo was not absolutely taken with a project he would eventually find a way to wriggle out of it.[12] Such statements may be interpreted as an expression of indifference or laziness from Pontecorvo. Or, given Pontecorvo's position in Italian society, perhaps he simply never felt the pecuniary urgency to make a film, with the possible exception of *Burn!* which apparently allowed him to purchase the apartment in a chic district of Rome where he spent his declining years.[13] Pontecorvo's financial station in the 1990s was secured when he accepted positions as director of the Venice Film Festival and president of Cinecittà Hold Spa, the state-owned company responsible for the management of the famed film studio complex in Rome.

But rather than pecuniary or artistic concerns and Pontecorvo's own explanations about feeling a sense of passion for potential projects, the answer to the question of whatever happened to Pontecorvo's directing career could have a historical interpretation. Pontecorvo's political and social ideals were forged during his years as a leader in the anti-Nazi/Fascist resistance in Italy during World War II. The experience of the intensity of an all-or-nothing struggle forged Pontecorvo's political consciousness with a sense of missionary idealism about resistance to oppression. Pontecorvo's films *Kapò* (1960), *The Battle of Algiers* (1966), and the undervalued *Burn!* (1966) sought to raise political and moral consciousness with allegorical depictions of events such as the Holocaust and historical issues such as colonialism and slavery. These films championed the legitimacy of active armed struggle against oppression, a logical extension of Pontecorvo's experiences in the anti-Nazi/Fascist resistance in World War II.

Even though his sympathies clearly lie with the underdog, ironically in Pontecorvo's films the antagonists often ring true to life and reach a level of communicative empathy uncommon in the political film genre, in which excessive rhetoric is a ready pitfall. Examples include Squarciò, the dynamite fisherman pursued by the police in *La grande strada azzurra/The Wide Blue Road* (1957); Edith, the Nazi work camp trustee who sacrifices herself so her fellow prisoners may escape in *Kapò* (1960); Mathieu, the former French resistance fighter who suppresses Algerian independence in *The Battle of Algiers* (1966); and Walker, the agent of the multinational sugar interests who struggles with his conscience while hunting down the rebel leader whom he helped to create in *Burn!* (1969). In these films Pontecorvo's antagonists present allegories of ideological struggles that are effective precisely because of the attention paid to the psychology of those on the losing side of history.

But by the time of his last feature, *Ogro/Operation Ogro*, Pontecorvo had lost the sense of duality between underdog and overlord that had been the fulcrum of his earlier productions and the certainty in his ideological convictions that had allowed him the courage to reveal opposing viewpoints. *Ogro*, in its depiction of the ETA assassination of Francoist minister Carrero Blanco, concentrates on divisions within the ETA terrorist cell rather than between the ETA terrorists and their Francoist adversaries. In fact in the film the victims of the ETA attack, Blanco and his entourage, appear only in church scenes, as static figures devoid of any depth. Pontecorvo's explanation for his half-hearted approach in *Ogro* is that the film was influenced by the events of 1978 in Italy, when left-wing terrorism shook the foundations of Italian society with the Red Brigade's kidnapping and murder of former Italian premier and Christian Democratic Party chair Aldo Moro. Pontecorvo later commented that *Ogro* was made with a guilty conscience, and that his previous interest in depicting the reasons and processes of armed struggled seemed inappropriate given concurrent events in Italy.[14] This attitude is particularly evident in the epilogue to *Ogro*, in which the ETA terrorists visit the deathbed of their most hard-line comrade and renounce political violence in favor of seeking change within democratic institutions. Given the political course taken by Spain after the death of Franco and the repercussions against violence after the murder of Moro in Italy, the film's epilogue is understandable.

When Pontecorvo retreated from active filmmaking he took positions in Italian cultural institutions, as the director of the Venice Film Festival and as president of Cinecittà Holding, a consortium that manages the famed film studios at Cinecittà in Rome. These two positions undoubtedly afforded Pontecorvo opportunities for professional development and financial security. During his creative retirement Pontecorvo also made some films for pecuniary reasons, including several commercials and a short for the Italian national petroleum company. But Pontecorvo's acceptance of bureaucratic postings cannot completely explain the break with creative filmmaking, particularly given the ideological fervor of his earlier productions. Despite the negative experience of *Ogro*, a director of Pontecorvo's caliber would have been expected to remain active in the political film genre. The question may be raised, particularly in consideration of his brilliantly influential, if somewhat limited, opus of completed work, What happened to Pontecorvo? And, by extension, what happened to the urgency and passion of his sense of political commitment? His artistic retreat raises the question of the ideological resonance and residue of his films. Are they too entangled with the political romanticism of the Cold War period to have a continuing relevance? Or should Pontecorvo's films offer an example of the path not taken by contemporary cinema despite his seeming denouement as a filmmaker? The answer may lie in analysis of the few films that Pontecorvo did complete after *Ogro*. He made a largely unknown documentary, *Il ritorno ad Algeri di Gillo Pontecorvo/Gillo Pontecorvo's Return to Algiers* (1992), which chronicles Pontecorvo's return to Algiers in 1991 to document his impressions of Algeria's struggle with civil war. Pontecorvo also made a short narrative film, *Nostalgia di protezione: Danza della fata confetto/Protection Nostalgia: Dance of the Sugar Plum Fairy* (1997) in which a Roman businessman frustrated with the petty incivility of modern life longs for the days of his boyhood, when he felt safe under the protective wing of his mother.

RETURN TO ALGIERS (1992)[15]

The West had its first introduction to the Franco-Algerian War through Pontecorvo's *The Battle of Algiers* (1966), a film that has since become not only a classic in the political film genre but reportedly a training film for both terrorist and antiterrorist organizations. *The Battle of Algiers* presents not only an interpretation of the historical events that led to Algerian independence but also the psychological motivations and organizational paradigms of a war in which terror was used by both sides. The film actually has two endings, each presenting a victory for the French and Algerian side. The end result is that the film rationalizes the recursion to violence and torture, so that it is quite understandable that the film has been used for the training of both terrorist organizations and counterinsurgency agencies.[16]

Pontecorvo had produced *The Battle of Algiers* himself in tandem with the Algerian government, and retained enough control of the production to be able to rigorously ensure that the film was made according to his artistic vision. The film is a striking example of Pontecorvo's ability to artificially re-create the neorealist style of the late 1940s. Like the Italian neorealists of the late 1940s, Pontecorvo shot the film on location with stock that gave a grainy texture to the film. He insisted on a story that emphasized social justice and political self-determination. Most importantly, he cast nonprofessional actors, most notably Brahim Haggiag, an illiterate nonprofessional actor whom Pontecorvo found in the streets, for the role of the protagonist, Ali Le Pointe. Pontecorvo also enjoyed remarkable collaboration from the Algerian government, with access to locations in the city of Algiers and its Casbah, and he was even able to call on the Algerian army for extras and props. The result was a film that had to be advertised as not containing any documentary footage because its first audiences simply assumed that it contained actual footage of the Algerian uprising, so gripping and stark was Pontecorvo's recreation of events.

In 1992, more than a quarter of a century after *The Battle of Algiers* was first released, Pontecorvo returned to Algeria to make the documentary that audiences had mistakenly assumed he had made nearly thirty years earlier. Pontecorvo was convinced to come out of artistic retirement by the Italian investigative television program *Mixer*, of the Italian state television RAI 2 channel, to chronicle and film his return trip to Algeria. The result was the documentary *Il ritorno in Algeri/Return in Algeria* (1992) with his son Marco

Pontecorvo serving as assistant director and photographer. The film is a running montage that alternates between footage of *The Battle of Algiers*, Pontecorvo doing man on the street interviews, and Pontecorvo discussing his vision of Algeria in the Roman studio of the Italian television network with Italian anchorman Gianni Minoli.

Pontecorvo was invited to go to Algiers because the theocratic Front of Islamic Salvation (FIS) party earned enough votes in the first multiparty elections ever held in Algeria to force a second round of voting and pose a serious electoral challenge to the socialist FLN, the party that had ousted the French colonialists and governed the country under single-party rule following independence. The reaction of the Algerian government and the FLN to this electoral embarrassment was to postpone the second round of elections due to the fear of a victory for the theocratic FIS. Pontecorvo's *Ritorno ad Algeri/Return to Algiers* is imbued with the awareness that the party that Pontecorvo championed in the mid-1960s had overturned a popular election. Thus the Algerian experiment with national self-determination and progress though reforms, whose genesis Pontecorvo had championed in *The Battle of Algiers*, had brought not peace and prosperity but rather a conflict between the ruling socialist secularists and Islamic theocrats who had previously unified forces to oust the French. If *The Battle of Algiers* was about the national liberation struggle against colonialism, *Return to Algiers* reveals the contradictions in the idealist vision that powered Pontecorvo's earlier feature films.

Return to Algiers opens with 1962 documentary footage of the French abandoning Algeria, with scenes of French civilians driving their cars onto waiting ferries followed by shots of popular jubilation following Algerian independence. Pontecorvo chose footage that in its tone and timbre recalled scenes of the liberation of Europe after World War II to the strains of heroic, celebratory music. The film then shifts to 1992 with the presentation of an Algeria on the verge of civil war after the postponed elections of 1991, with scenes of street violence and repression by government troops. The fact that the Algerian government was forced to cancel the second round of elections that would have resulted in its defeat posed a difficult dilemma for Western intelligentsia. In the documentary Pontecorvo provides an initial explanation by returning to a terrace where he filmed a sequence for *The Battle of Algiers* twenty-six years earlier. In the scene Ben M'hidi, the historical leader of the FLN, tells the actor playing the anti-French fighter Ali Le Pointe that it may seem difficult to start a revolution but that it is even more problematic to continue one. He concludes that the true difficulties for Algeria will begin after the French depart. Pontecorvo, who appears in his documentary *Return to Algiers* as narrator and interviewer, comments on the prophetic validity of

Ben M'hidi's statement by insisting that Ben M'hidi should have added, "above all if we are not able to follow the path of freedom and democracy."

Pontecorvo's initial statement seems to be an indication of a lack of appreciation of the theocratic threat faced by the FLN regime. The results of the 1991 election that brought a victory for the theocratic FIS were part of a political current that in the last quarter of the twentieth century brought theocratic regimes to countries such as Afghanistan, Iran, and Somalia. The unfortunate conclusion is that the Algerian Republic, with its ideological grounding in Nasserite pan-Arab socialism, did not foster a political situation that the Algerian socialists of the FLN and Westerners like Pontecorvo expected after the struggle for independence so dramatically portrayed in *The Battle of Algiers*. When Pontecorvo appears on camera in his documentary and attempts to answer the question of whether the Algerian government was correct to suspend elections after the victory of the theocratic FIS party, he states that it was the choice of a lesser evil. If forced to choose between the plague (theocratic rule) and cholera (suspension of free elections), the only rational choice is the latter. The film also includes excerpts from an interview Pontecorvo conducted with Mohamed Boudiaf, the head of the provisional government who was assassinated shortly after the making of Pontecorvo's film. When Pontecorvo asks Boudiaf questions about the future of democratic rule in Algeria, Boudiaf confirms Pontecorvo's analysis by stating that any semblance of democratic institutions in Algeria would not have survived an electoral victory for the theocratic FIS.

In support of his analysis of events, Pontecorvo's documentary contains a segment presenting the successes of the Algerian government since the departure of the French. These include the development of a compulsory education system within ten years of independence, the establishment of public universities twenty years after the departure of the French, and a foreign policy of participation in the nonaligned movement. To his credit in his commentary Pontecorvo points out that the spirit of the independence movement gave way to one-party rule and the inevitable corruption typical of authoritarian regimes. In the 1980s Algeria's demographic explosion coincided with a worldwide drop in oil prices, the main source of revenue for the state, and mass riots occurred in 1988. After attempts to quell dissension, the FLN announced in February of 1989 that it would allow other political parties and free elections, a statement that Pontecorvo comments was not entirely believed by the general populace. However, rather than the development of political parties in a manner that a Westerner like Pontecorvo might expect, the FLN's political opening led to the rise of the theocratic FIS. Due to the fact that there are thousands of mosques in Algeria, the theocratic FIS was well positioned to channel discontent into political power, which led to its stunning victory in the first round of elections in 1991. When Pontecorvo attempts to face the difficult question of what happened to Algiers since he made *The Battle of Algiers* in 1966, he compares situation in Algeria to that of Eastern Bloc. Pontecorvo's analysis is perhaps to be expected, given that the film was made shortly after the implosion of the Soviet empire.

However, the question of what happened in Algeria after independence is answered more effectively in the documentary by the images Pontecorvo shows of Algeria than by his commentary. Besides a presentation of the political situation in Algeria, the film features segments in which Pontecorvo takes on the role of street journalist after the pulse of the Algerian people. The startling aspect of these man on the street interviews is the initial level of hostility displayed against Pontecorvo, who, at least in the West, enjoys a reputation for being a champion of the common man. For example, Pontecorvo and his documentary crew visit the prison where the opening scenes of *The Battle of Algiers* were shot. The documentary shifts from a full shot of Pontecorvo in the prison to the scene from *The Battle of Algiers* in which a condemned man being led to guillotine incites the passions of his fellow prisoners by yelling "Long live Algeria." The scene climaxes in a zoom on the angry eyes of Ali Le Pointe from the barred window of his cell, with the sound of the guillotine falling on the condemned man's neck. Pontecorvo reports that when he filmed the guillotine scene the prison was empty after the French had abandoned the country. Now with the country on the brink of civil war, the prison holds approximately five thousand political prisoners, a number Pontecorvo comments is quite small, considering the level of political chaos in the country. In another segment of the documentary Pontecorvo presents footage of the bodies of eight policemen whose station was attacked in broad daylight by theocratic guerillas. The scenes recall a sequence from *The Battle of Algiers* in which FLN commandos break into a French colonial police station and commit a similar massacre. Pontecorvo does not play this scene from *The Battle of Algiers* in his documentary, despite the ironic parallel between the methods of the FIS and the FLN nearly thirty years prior. Another irony in the documentary is that when Pontecorvo visits the old French quarter he reports that it has since become the stronghold of the FIS. It is at this point in the documentary that Pontecorvo reveals the depth of the hostility of the FIS supporters, who spit at Pontecorvo and verbally abuse him and his film crew. In a voice-over Pontecorvo admits that he was advised to leave before his presence provoked an outbreak of violence. In Pontecorvo's few exchanges with FIS supporters he is told that in their view all foreign journalists are aligned with the government. Pontecorvo made a name for himself by representing the oppressed, but upon his return to Algeria he is seen by the FIS opposition as a pawn of the FLN status quo.

Pontecorvo also visits one of the public universities whose existence he claims is one of the great achievements of the regime. Pontecorvo relates that when making *The Battle of Algiers* he and his crew had come to the university to recruit extras as French paratroopers, looking in particular for members of the Kabili ethnic minority. At the university Pontecorvo's presence incites a violent argument between FIS and FLN supporters. A particularly strident protheocratic student advises Pontecorvo to leave and warns other students not to talk about Algeria's problems in front of a foreigner. The phrase the student uses to explain himself is translated into Italian as the proverb "I panni sporchi si lavano in famiglia" (Dirty linen must not be washed in public). There is a heavy irony in the use of such a proverb for Pontecorvo, who used nonprofessional actors and on-location shooting in homage to the famed Italian neorealist style. The proverb about not washing dirty linen in public was used in Italy in the late 1940s by then minister Giulio Andreotti to explain the denial of government subvention for Vittorio De Sica's films like *Umberto D.* (1952), which Andreotti felt portrayed a negative image of Italy.

Pontecorvo argues with the protheocratic student and tries to convince the student of his good intentions, that he is on the side of the common man, but to no avail. Pontecorvo receives a hostile repetition that recalls the earlier scenes when his crew visited the former French quarter of the city, now an FIS stronghold. In his role as street journalist Pontecorvo explains the hatred of the Western media that he encountered in Algeria and the level of intolerance evident in theocratic culture by citing how in centuries past Islam allowed a certain level of religious plurality. Pontecorvo cites Voltaire's *Treatise on Tolerance* (1763), which reports that in the eighteenth century the Turkish sultan was far more tolerant than his Christian counterparts. Again the images that Pontecorvo shows of Algeria are more convincing than his comments. Pontecorvo follows the scene of intolerance at the public university with a presentation of the level of religious education of young Algerians, whose main form of education consists of memorization of the Koran in crowded rooms. Pontecorvo displays extended shots of innocents repeating verses with pans of the turrets of mosques and the hardened faces of adults. However Pontecorvo wisely insists that it is dangerous to reduce Islam to terrorism, backwardness, and intolerance. Echoing Edward Said, he explains the violence of the protheocratic followers in Algeria as residual of colonialism. He supports this point with interviews of Western-dressed Algerian women who decry the severity against women of theocratic law, which requires punishments like lapidation for not following the dictates of Islamic legal codes. However when Pontecorvo asks the same women about the first Gulf War of 1991, a recent event at the time, they affirm their support for Iraqi dictator Saddam Hussein out of a sense of pan-Arabic racial solidarity and claim that the Gulf War brought many university-educated women to wear the veil as a symbol of resistance against the West.

The most important aspect of the documentary is the amount of attention that Pontecorvo pays to women's issues. This was also a central theme of his feature films, such as *Giovanna* (1955), which depicts the strike of women at a textile factory, and *Kapò* (1960), which develops the topic of the Holocaust through the moral and political consciousness of a Parisian girl deported to the Nazi concentration camps who becomes a trustee or kapò. In the documentary Pontecorvo interviews a group of veiled high school girls who tell him they hope coeducational classrooms will be abolished. These seemingly retroactive attitudes of young Algerians are underscored by interviews of Western-dressed Algerian women who explain that in a theocratic society a woman must have a male sponsor to get married, since legally women are life-long minors without the same civil rights as males. When Pontecorvo asks the obvious question of why anyone would desire inferior civil status, the answer he receives is that such attitudes are the result of societal pressures and tradition. According to the women he interviews, some Algerian women prefer living according to the customs of traditional society. Pontecorvo's documentary effectively intercuts these interviews, mostly done in interior settings where women felt comfortable enough to voice their opinions, with statements from men on the street who support the FIS because they claim it represents the views of most Algerians.

With his examination of women's issues, Pontecorvo presents the political conflict between the FIS and the Algerian government as a struggle between two Algerias, one traditional and the other close to the West. Pontecorvo makes the revelatory statement that what ultimately separates the West from the Islamic world is the West's inability to understand the Islamic world's conception of the male-female divide. Pontecorvo explains that in Algeria women's rights activists have little influence in Algerian politics and live under constant threat of violence from the theocratic factions. According to Pontecorvo, the majority of women accept the situation because of the existence of a female zone in Algerian society with separate social activities, including separate funeral celebrations, which Pontecorvo includes in the documentary.

To prove his points further Pontecorvo visits one of the large courtyards of the Casbah, which he reports become a zone of female control during the workday. In the Casbah Pontecorvo returns to set locations chosen from *The Battle of Algiers*. Pontecorvo explains how the Franco-Algerian conflict developed in the Casbah. In his analysis the war for independence was initially a conflict between uniformed French soldiers and guerillas that escalated after procolonial paramilitary groups such as the OAS planted bombs in the Casbah. The documentary cuts to a scene from *The Battle of Algiers* of the aftermath of a bomb blast in the Casbah, with sacred music accompanying shots of the body of a dead child being taken from the rubble. Pontecorvo follows this scene of a French atrocity from *The Battle of Algiers* with a sequence from the film depicting an FLN atrocity in which Algerian women dressed in Western garb plant a bomb at a bar packed with dancing teenagers in the French quarter. As mentioned before, Pontecorvo's strength as a director is his ability to show all sides of the issues and the suffering of innocents caused by a conflict. However, Pontecorvo's visit to the Casbah is also marked by the hostility that he was shown at the university and the old French quarter. Pontecorvo's documentary opens the Casbah sequence with shots of children playing and an elderly woman complaining about government inattention to the needs of the Casbah. However, when Pontecorvo asks the women if they feel oppressed, if they accept the situation of women in Algeria, he eventually receives the same hostile reaction he had experienced at the public university and in the old French quarter. He is asked if he is authorized by the state to film in the Casbah, word spreads of his presence, and his film crew must retreat to the safety of their van.

The documentary ends with an interview Pontecorvo conducted with the then president of Algeria, Boudiaf. Pontecorvo asks about the unkept promises of independence, the reasons why people voted FIS, and possible solutions to the crisis. The president answers in diplomatic tones that Pontecorvo seconds, adding that in his opinion the FIS is a protest movement, an expression of popular discontent. Of course the irony is that Pontecorvo's former colleagues of the FLN were in the position of opposing democratic elections that might lead to their defeat. In this vein perhaps the ultimate message of Pontecorvo's *Return to Algiers* is an expression of *trasformismo*, the idea of a sense of fatalism regarding Italian politics popularized by Tomasi de Lampedusa in his novel *Il Gattopardo/The Leopard.* In a discussion in the novel about the future of Sicily in a newly unified Italy in the 1870s, a Sicilian count claims that despite outward appearances nothing in Sicily will change—the more things change the more they stay the same. Despite the FLN's attempts to introduce Western-style reforms in Algeria—which Pontecorvo proudly lists, such as public education and public universities—the country remains deeply divided as Algerian society struggles with the legacy of tribal and theocratic customs most evident in the social status of women.

Pontecorvo's documentary is a testimony to the incomprehension between the West and the Islamic world. However, what is most striking about Pontecorvo's film is that he no longer seems to propose the sort of ideologically rigorous defense or advocacy of armed struggle that characterized his feature films. Pontecorvo's cinematic and political culture was founded in the tenets of neorealism and the Italian resistance. In *The Battle of Algiers* Pontecorvo relied on his background as a resistance fighter to portray the Algerian struggle for independence for a Western audience. However, when he returned twenty-six years later his documentary revealed a country struggling with a threat from theocratic retroactivity, and Pontecorvo's cinematic and political points of reference, neorealism and the Italian resistance, were not as clearly applicable to the coming Algerian civil struggle of the 1990s as they had been to the Algerian struggle for independence in the 1950s.

NOSTALGIA DI PROTEZIONE: DANZA DELLA FATA CONFETTO/PROTECTION NOSTALGIA: THE NUTCRACKER SUITE (1997)

If a spirit of fatalism pervades *Return to Algiers*, Pontecorvo's next and possibly his last short narrative, *Protection Nostalgia* (1997), is a full retreat into a microcosm of nostalgia. Pontecorvo began his directing career by making short narrative films that in the 1950s were eligible for Italian government grants because cinema houses were required to screen shorts between features. Pontecorvo made several films in the neorealist style common in the period. *Porta portese/Portese Gate* (1954) depicts haggling at the vast Roman flea market. *Cani dietro le sbarre/Dogs behind Bars* (1955) is a look at the plight of stray dogs in Roman dog kennels. *Pane e zolfe/Bread and Sulfur* (1959) documents the effects of the closing of a sulfur mine on a small Italian town. *Protection Nostalgia* may have been a return to Pontecorvo's early roots as a director. However, despite being a short, the film has a larger scope than a neorealist style exposé of social ills. The film seems to be Pontecorvo's testament, a melancholy take on human nature, with the same sense of fatalism that pervades *Return to Algiers*.

The film opens with scenes of a Roman traffic jam. A businessman, played by Fabrizio Bentivoglio, curses motorists who beep their horns. He leaves the chaotic Roman streets and enters a conference room where his colleagues, like the motorists before, complain and argue, which Pontecorvo presents with an overhead shot. The businessman exits the room and seeks the company of his secretary, played by Valeria Golino. When she asks him how the meeting is proceeding, he answers in a depressed tone that he is weary of the petty disagreements, personal infighting, and the useless aggression of life. The man sighs and laments that everything seems to be getting worse everyday. She reminds him that he also is known to have a difficult character and that perhaps he should realize that the aggression he finds annoying in others, he forgives in himself. Back at his desk, after arguing on the phone, he comments that he would like to spend some time with his son, who is away on vacation with his wife, a possible allusion to marital separation. The man returns to the street for a stroll, but passing cars block his path. He goes to a park, where he sees children playing. But instead of peaceful scenes of childhood innocence he witnesses a boy bullying a smaller child, who runs to the safety of his mother. When the mother comforts the child, a subjective camera shot of the businessman's point of view dissolves into a flashback of his recollections of his mother picking him up at school, with a sound track of the music of the "Dance of the Sugar Plum Fairies" from Tchaikovsky's *Nutcracker Suite*. The flashback continues with images of the mother, played by Isabella Ferrari, tucking the boy into bed the night before Epiphany, the traditional date when gifts are exchanged following Christmas in parts of Italy, including Rome. The boy protests that he does want to sleep until the arrival of the *befana* (the good witch of Epiphany). The mother admonishes him that the *befana* never visits children who do not fall asleep. After his mother leaves, the child sneaks out of bed to the *Nutcracker* theme, goes down the hall, and turns on a light to see his stocking hanging from a chandelier. The flashback ends with an image of the boy innocently reaching for his stocking. The film then shifts back to the present, when the man encounters a jogger who disdainfully emits the same sort of colorful expression that the businessman had used to refer to the drivers annoying him in the traffic jam in the opening scene of the film.

The film, probably Pontecorvo's last venture into narrative filmmaking, was largely ignored by both critics and public and not well received at the few film festivals where it was screened. Audiences perhaps did not expect such a personal film from a director with Pontecorvo's reputation for political filmmaking. *Protection Nostalgia* expresses a sense of yearning for the only time when a person feels truly safe, under a mother's protection. The film could simply be an expression of the *mammismo*, mamma's boy syndrome, for which Italians are stereotypically famous. But rather than maudlin *mammismo*, the circular narrative structure of the film is imbued with a sense of fatalism about human nature that echoes the tone of *Return to Algiers*. *Protection Nostalgia* points out the hypocrisy of a man able to see the fault of aggression in his peers but not in himself. The short also begins and ends with a presentation of the eternal cycle of petty incivility, first between strangers in a Roman traffic jam, then in a business meeting, then among children, and finally on the street between a pedestrian and a jogger. On the surface with this short film Pontecorvo seems to have retreated into the microcosm of personal recollection, with a sense of impotence about the unresolved and perhaps irresolvable failings in human nature. It is a film that is completely opposite in tone and in theme to the sense of ideological struggle of Pontecorvo's feature films of the 1950s and 1960s. The earlier films focus on themes of collective responsibility; when he made them Pontecorvo was a prime exponent of a cinematic culture based on a desire to depict the ills of the world in order to foster a sense of moral consciousness and solidarity. With both *Return to Algiers* and *Protection Nostalgia* Pontecorvo confirms his sense of doubt regarding the efficacy of political violence promoted in *The Battle of Algiers* (1966) and *Burn!* (1969), which he later questioned in the epilogue of *Ogro* (1979). In this context Pontecorvo's last two films are not evidence of ideological decline but rather are a fruition of the lessons he learned previously. His last two films indicate that his withdrawal from feature filmmaking might be an act of deliberate separation from his earlier work. If Pontecorvo's work is taken as a whole, from the neorealist themes of *Giovanna* (1956) to the retreating tone of *Protection Nostalgia* (1997), the story of Pontecorvo's films is not one of ideological decline, but rather one of arrival at maturity and acceptance of the frailties of human nature.

NOTES

1. Irene Bignardi, *Memorie estorte a uno smemorato vita di Gillo Pontecorvo* (Milan: Feltrinelli, 1999), 162–78.
2. Bignardi, *Memorie*.
3. Bignardi, *Memorie*.
4. Aldo Tassone, *Parla il Cinema Italiano*, 1st vol. (Paris: Edilig, 1982), 227.
5. Bignardi, *Memorie*.
6. Gillo Pontecorvo, "Intervista," *Queimada!* (Rome: Eagle Pictures, 2003).
7. Luigi Cipriani, M. Conciatori, M. Giraldi, and L. Ricci, eds., *Primo piano sull'autore Gillo Pontecorvo "La dittatura della verità"* (Rome: Designer, 1999), 22.
8. Christopher Frayling, *Spaghetti Westerns: Cowboys and Europeans from Karl May to Sergio Leone* (London: I. B. Tauris, 1998).
9. Bignardi, *Memorie*.
10. Bignardi, *Memorie*.
11. Bignardi, *Memorie*.
12. Bignardi, *Memorie*.
13. Bignardi, *Memorie*.
14. Bignardi, *Memorie*, 161–91.
15. An earlier version of this review was published as Carlo Celli, "Gillo Pontecorvo's *Return to Algiers (1992)*," *Film Quarterly* 58, no. 2 (Winter 2004–2005): 49–53.
16. Stuart Klawans, "Lessons of the Pentagon's Favorite Training Film," *New York Times*, January 4, 2004, 26.

Filmography[1]

Il sole sorge ancora/Outcry, 1946, 90 minutes
Director: Aldo Vergano
Cast: Elli Parvo (Donna Matilda), Massimo Serato (Major Heinrich), Lea
  Padovani (Laura), Vittorio Duse (Cesare), Carlo Lizzani (Don Camillo),
  Gillo Pontecorvo (Pietro), Checco Rissone (Mario), Aldo Vergano
  (railroad worker), Alfonso Gatto (conductor), Lia Golmar (Matilda's
  cousin), Giuseppe De Santis (servant), Egisto Olivieri (Laura's father),
  Marco Sarri (Cesare's brother)
Screenplay: Giuseppe Gorgerino (story), Guido Aristarco, Giuseppe De
  Santis, Carlo Lizzani, Aldo Vergano
Music: Giuseppe Rosati
Cinematography: Aldo Tonti
Editing: Gabriele Varriale
Sets: Fausto Gallil
Costumes: Anna Gobbi
Producer: Giorgio Agliani

DOCUMENTARIES/SHORTS

La Missione Timiriazev/The Timiriazev Mission (1953)
Porta Portese/Portese Gate (1954)
Festa a Castelluccio/Festival at Castelluccio (1954)

Cani dietro le sbarre/Dogs behind Bars (1955)
Pane e zolfo/Bread and Sulfur (1956)
L'Addio a Enrico Berlinguer/Farewell to Enrico Berlinguer (multiple directors) (1984)
Una storia per l'energia/An Energy Story (1984)
Una doppia assenza: Immagini sul lavoro femminile nell'industira (1987)
12 registi per 12 città/12 Directors for 12 Cities (1989) ("Udine" segment)
Il ritorno ad Algeri di Gillo Pontecorvo/Gillo Pontecorvo's Return to Algiers (1992)
Un altro mondo è possibile/Another World Is Possible (2001)
Nostalgia di protezione: Danza della fata confetto/Protection Nostalgia: Dance of the Sugar Plum Fairy (1997)
Firenze, il nostro domani/Florence, Our Tomorrow (2003)

FEATURES

Giovanna, 1956, 36-minute episode in *Die Winderose/Rose of the Winds*, by Joris Ivens
Director: Gillo Pontecorvo
Cast: Armida Gianassi (Giovanna), Carla Pozzi
Screenplay: Franco Solinas
Photogtaphy: Erico Menczer
Editing: Enzo Alfonzi
Costumes: Elena Mannini
Music: Mario Zafred

La grande strada azzurra/The Wide Blue Road, 1956, 100 minutes
Director: Gillo Pontecorvo
Cast: Yves Montand (Squarciò), Alida Valli (Rosetta), Francisco Rabal (Salvatore), Umberto Spadaro (Gaspar Puggioni, first Coast Guard Officer), Peter Carsten (Riva, second Coast Guard Officer), Federica Ranchi (Diana), Terence Hill Mario Girotti (Renato), Ronaldo Bonacchi (Bore), Giancarlo Soblone (Tonino), Josip Batistic, Stane Potokar, Angelo Zanolli, Giorgio Kuru, Janez Vrhovec, Milutin Jasnic, Angela Sarlone, Pasquale Campagnola
Screenplay: Gillo Pontecorvo, Franco Solinas
Music: Carlo Franci
Cinematography: Montuori
Editing: Eraldo Da Roma

Costumes: Lucia Mirisola
Producer: Maleno Malenotti

Kapò, 1959, 135 minutes
Director: Gillo Pontecorvo
Cast: Susan Strasberg (Edith/Nicole), Laurent Terzieff (Sascha), Em-
manuelle Riva (Terese), Didi Perego (Sofia), Gianni Garko (Karl),
Eleonora Bellinzaghi, Annabella Besi, Mira Dinulovic, Mirjana Dojc,
Dragomir Felba, Graziella Galvani, Paola Pitagora, Bruno Scipioni
Screenplay: Gillo Pontecorvo, Franco Solinas
Music: Carlo Rustichelli
Cinematography: Goffredo Bellisario, Marcello Gatti, Marco Scarpelli, Alek-
sandar Sekulovic
Editing: Roberto Cinquini
Art Direction: Piero Gherardi
Producer: Moris Ergas

La battaglia di Algeri/ The Battle of Algiers, 1966, 123 minutes
Director: Gillo Pontecorvo
Cast: Brahim Haggiag (Ali La Pointe), Jean Martin (Colonel Mathieu), Yacef
Saadi (Djafar), Samia Kerbash, Ugo Paletti (Captain), Fusia El Kader
(Halima), Mohamed Ben Kassen (Petit Omar), Michele Kerbash
(Fathia), Franco Morici Tommaso Neri, Gene Wesson
Screenplay: Gillo Pontecorvo, Franco Solinas, Yacef Saadi
Music: Ennio Morricone, Gillo Pontecorvo
Cinematography: Marcello Gatti
Editing: Mario Morra, Mario Serandrei
Assistant Directors: Moussa Haddad, Giuliano Montaldo, Fernando
Morandi
Producers: Antonio Musu (Igor Film Italy), Yacef Saadi, Casbah Algeria

Queimada!/Burn! 1969, 112 minutes
Director: Gillo Pontecorvo
Cast: Marlon Brando (Sir William Walker), Evaristo Márquez (Jose Do-
lores), Norman Hill (Shelton), Renato Salvatori (Teddy Sanchez), Dana
Ghia (Francesca), Valeria Ferran Wanani (Guarina), Giampiero Alber-
tini (Henry), Carlo Palmucci (Jack), Thomas Lyons (General Prada),
Joseph P. Persaud (Juanito), Álvaro Medrano, Alejandro Obregón (Ma-
jor), Cecily Browne Laird (Lady Bella), Maurice Rodriguez (Ramon)
Screenplay: Franco Solinas, Giorgio Arlorio
Music: Ennio Morricone

Cinematography: Marcello Gatti, Giuseppe Ruzzolini
Editing: Mario Morra
Production Design: Sergio Canevari
Costumes: Marilù Carteny
Assistant Director: Salvatore Basile, Rinaldo Ricci
Producer: Alberto Grimaldi

Ogro/Operation Ogre—The Tunnel, 1979, 115 minutes
Director: Gillo Pontecorvo
Cast: Gian Maria Volonté (Izarra), José Sacristán (Icar), Ángela Molina
(Amayore), Eusebio Poncela (Txabi), Saverio Marconi (Luque), Georges
Staquet (El Albañil), Nicole Garcia (Karmele), Féodor Atkine (José
María Uriarte (alias Joseba), Estanis González, Agapito Romo, José
Manuel Cervino, José Luis Pérez, Luis Politti (Spanish professor),
Agustín Navarro, Ana Torrent (Basque girl)
Screenplay: Giorgio Arlorio, Ugo Pirro, Gillo Pontecorvo
Music: Ennio Morricone
Cinematography: Marcello Gatti

NOTE

1. Sources for the filmography include www.imdb.com; Irene Bignardi, *Memorie di
uno smemorato vita di Gillo Pontecorvo* (Milan: Feltrinelli, 1999); Massimo Ghirelli, *Gillo
Pontecorvo* (Firenze, Italy: La Nuova Italia, 1978); and Luigi Cirpiani, M. Conciatori,
M. Giraldi, and L. Ricci, *Primo piano sull'autore Gillo Pontecorvo "La dittatura della verità"* (Rome: Designer, 1999).

Bibliography

Agirre, Julen. *Operation Ogro: The Execution of Admiral Luis Carrero Blanco.* Trans. Barbara Probost Soloman. New York: Quadrangle/New York Times, 1975.

Aprà, Adriano, and Riccardo Redi, eds. *Sole: Soggetto, sceneggiatura, note per la realizzazione.* Rome: Di Giacomo, 1985.

Bakhtin, Mikhail. *Rabelais and His World.* Trans. Helene Iswolsky. Bloomington: Indiana University Press, 1984.

Baroni, Maurizio. *Platea in piedi, 1945–1958: Manifesti e dati statistici del cinema italiano; Testi a cura di Valerio M. Manfredi.* Bologna, Italy: Bolelli Editore, 1995–1999.

Bignardi, Irene. "The Making of Battle of Algiers." *Cineaste* 25, no. 2 (2000): 14–22.

———. *Memorie di uno smemorato vita di Gillo Pontecorvo.* Milan: Feltrinelli, 1999.

Black, Gregory D. *The Catholic Crusade against the Movies 1940–1975.* Cambridge: Cambridge University Press, 1977.

Blasetti, Alessandro. *Il cinema che ho vissuto.* Ed. Franco Prono. Bari, Italy: Edizioni dedalo, 1982.

Bolzoni, Francesco, and M. Foglietti. *Le stagioni del cinema.* Catanzaro, Italy: Rubbettino, 2000.

Brombert, Victor. *The Intellectual Hero: Studies in the French Novel, 1880–1955.* Chicago: University of Chicago Press, 1960.

Brunetta, Gian Piero. *Guida alla storia del cinema italiano, 1905–2003.* Turin, Italy: Einaudi, 2003.

Burlingame, Jon, and Gary Crowdus. "Music at the Service of the Cinema: An Interview with Ennio Morricone." *Cineaste* 21, no. 1–2 (1995): 76–80.

Casadio, Gianfranco. *Adultere, Fedifraghe, Innocenti: La donna del "neorealismo popolare" nel cinema italiano degli anni Cinquanta.* Ravenna, Italy: Longo Editore, 1990.

———. *Il grigio e il nero: Spettacolo e propaganda nel cinema italiano degli anni Trenta (1931–1943).* Ravenna, Italy: Longo, 1989.

Celli, Carlo. "Aldo Vergano's *Il sole sorge ancora/Outcry* (1946) as Influence on Gillo Pontecorvo." *Forum Italicum* 38, no. 1 (Spring 2004): 217–28.

———. "Alessandro Blasetti and Representations of Italian Fascism in the 1930s." *Italian Culture* 16, no. 2 (1998): 99–109.

———. "Critical and Philosophical Discussions regarding Italian Neo-Realism." *Romance Languages Annual* 7 (1995): 222–26.

———. *The Divine Comic: The Cinema of Roberto Benigni*. Lanham, MD: Scarecrow, 2001.

———. "Gillo Pontecorvo's *Return to Algiers* (1992)." *Film Quarterly* 58, no. 2 (2004): 49–52.

———. "Interview with Marcello Pezzetti." *Critical Inquiry* 27 (Autumn 2000): 149–57.

———. "Italian Neorealism's Wartime Legacy: Roberto Rossellini's *Rome Open City* and *Man of the Cross*." *Romance Languages Annual* 10 (1998): 225–28.

———. "The Legacy of the Films of Mario Camerini in Vittorio De Sica's *Ladri di biciclette/The Bicycle Thief* (1948)." *Cinema Journal* 40, no. 4 (2001): 3–17.

———. "A Lost De Sica Film—*La porta del cielo/The Gate of Heaven* (1945)." *Quarterly Review of Film and Video* 18, no. 4: 361–70.

———. "A Master Narrative in Italian Cinema?" *Italica* 81, no. 1 (2004): 73–83.

———. "The Representation of Evil in Roberto Benigni's *La vita è bella/Life Is Beautiful*." *Journal of Popular Film and Television* 28, no. 2 (Summer 2000): 74–79.

Chiti, Roberto, and Enrico Lancia. *Dizionario del cinema italiano: I Film vol. 1, dal 1930 al 1944*. Rome: Gremese, 1993.

Cirpiani, Luigi, M. Conciatori, M. Giraldi, and L. Ricci, eds. *Primo piano sull'autore Gillo Pontecorvo "La dittatura della verità."* Rome: Designer, 1999.

Clark, Robert P. *The Basque Insurgents: ETA, 1952–1980*. Madison: University of Wisconsin Press, 1984.

Clawson, Mary Ann. "Veiled Agents: Feminine Agency and Masquerade in *The Battle of Algiers*." In *Negotiating at the Margins: The Gendered Discourses of Power and Resistance*. New Brunswick, NJ: Rutgers University Press, 1993.

Collotti, Enzo. *Il fascismo e gli ebrei: Le leggi razziali in Italia*. Roma: Laterza, 2003.

"Contenuti extra," *Ogro* DVD. Rome: Cristaldi Film, 2003.

Cook, Pam. *The Cinema Book: A Complete Guide to Understanding the Movies*. New York: Pantheon, 1985.

Cottino-Jones, Marga. *A Student's Guide to Italian Cinema*. Dubuque, IA: Kendall Hunt, 1992.

Covington, Francee. "Are the Revolutionary Techniques Employed in *The Battle of Algiers* Applicable to Harlem?" In *The Black Woman*, ed. Toni Cade Bambara, 244–51. New York: New American Library, 1970.

Crenshaw, Martha. "The Causes of Terrorism." *Comparative Politics* 13, no. 4 (July, 1981): 379–99.

Crowdus, Gary, and Dan Georgakas. "Acting and the Collective Filmmaking Experience: An Interview with Gian Maria Volonte." in *Cineaste* 15, no. 1 (1986): 9–11.

Crowther, Bosley. "*The Battle of Algiers*." *New York Times*, September 23, 1967.

Curtis, Oliver. *Pontecorvo: The Dictatorship of Truth*. Channel Four (Great Britain); Cinema Guild, 1992.

De Lazzari, Primo. *Storia del Fronte della gioventù nella Resistenza, 1943–1945*. Milan: Mursia, 1996.

Desowitz, Bill. "Gillo Pontecorvo: An Early Document from a True Radical." *New York Times*, June 3, 2001.

Dine, Philip. *Images of the Algerian War: French Fiction and Film, 1954–1992.* Oxford: Claredon, 1994.

Doane, Mary Ann. *The Desire to Desire the Women's Film in the 1940s.* Bloomington, IN: Indiana University Press, 1987.

Faldini, Franca, and Goffredo Fofi, eds. *L'Avventurosa storia del cinema Italian raccontata dai suoi protagonisti, 1935–1959.* Milan: Feltrinelli, 1979.

Fanon, Frantz. *A Dying Colonialism.* New York: Grove, 1967.

———. *The Wretched of the Earth.* New York: Grove, 1966.

Ferrero, Adelio. "Queimada di Gillo Ponetcorvo." *Mondo Nuovo* 6 (February 1970).

Fofi, Goffredo. "La Battaglia di Algeri." In *Duecento Film Prima e Dopo il Sessantotto.* Milan: Felttrini, 1977.

Francione, Fabio. *Il coraggio delle idee: Gillo Pontecorvo intelletuale e cineasta cosmopolita.* Santhia, Italy: Grafica Santieatese Editrice, 2000.

Frayling, Christopher. *Spaghetti Westerns: Cowboys and Europeans from Karl May to Sergio Leone.* London: I. B. Tauris, 1998.

Furhammar, Leif, and Folke Isaksson. *Politics and Film.* New York: Preager, 1971.

Fusco, Maria Pia. "Pontecorvo e la nostalgia torna a Venezia con il suo nuovo film Corto." *La repubblica,* August 24, 1997.

Ghirelli, Massimo. *Gillo Pontecorvo.* Firenze, Italy: La Nuova Italia, 1978.

Gill, Brendan. "Truthtelling." *New Yorker,* September 23, 1967, 93.

Glass, Charlie. "The Hour of the Birth of Death: Pontecorvo's Long Silence and the Demise of Political Film-making." *Times Literary Supplement,* June 28, 1998.

Gori, Gianfranco. *Alessandro Blasetti.* Firenze, Italy: La Nuova Italia, 1984.

Hartung, Phillip T. "So Long at the Festival." *Commonweal,* October 20, 1967.

Heiberg, Marianne. *The Making of the Basque Nation.* New York: Cambridge University Press, 1989.

Holden, Stephen. "If He Had Been a Comrade, He Could've Been a Contender." *New York Times,* June 6, 2001, B1.

Hunter, Stephen. "Fishing for Trouble in 'The Wide Blue Road.'" *Washington Post,* November 9, 2001, C5.

The Internet Movie Database, www.imdb.com.

Kaufman, Stanley. "Recent Wars." *New Republic,* December 16, 1967.

Kennedy, Patrick. "One Deadly Summit." *Sight and Sound,* 2001, 28–29.

Kieslowski, Krysztof, K. Piesiewicz, G. Pontecorvo, M. Fabbri. *Tre colori: Blu, bianco, rosso.* Milan: Bompiani, 1994.

Klawans, Stuart. "Lessons of the Pentagon's Favorite Training Film." *New York Times,* January 4, 2004, 26.

Kolotowitz, Robert. "New Films: Adultery, Murder, and a Big Revolution." *Harpers,* December 1967, 133.

Kozlof, Max. "Shooting at Wars: Three Views." *Film Quarterly,* Winter 1967–1968, 27–29.

Lapid, Joseph. "Pontecorvo's Jesus as Working Man vs. Jewish and Roman Rulers." *Variety,* July 25, 1972, 3.

Leoni, Fausta. *Karma: Storia autentica di una reincarnazione.* Rome: Edizioni Mediterranee, 1979.

Letizia, Lorenzo. *Lezioni di regia: Conversazioni con Cavani, Lizzani, Guédiguian, Pontecorvo, Vancini.* Turin, Italy: Lindau, 2004.

Levi, Primo. *Survival in Auschwitz: The Nazi Assault on Humanity.* Trans. Stuart Woolf. New York: Collier Books, 1959.

Lucas, Corinne. "Political Terrorism in *Ogro*: An Interview with Gillo Pontecorvo." In *The Cineaste Interviews on the Art and Politics of the Cinema.* Ed. Dan Georgakas and Lenny Rubenstein, 307–12. Chicago: Lake View, 1983.

Mafai, Miriam. *Il lungo freddo: Storia di Bruno Pontecorvo, lo scienzato che scelse l'URSS.* Milan: A. Mondadori, 1992.

Massu, Jacques. *La vraie bataille d'Alger.* Paris: Plon, 1971.

Medici, Antonio. *Gillo Pontecorvo Giovanna: Storia di un film e del suo restauro.* Rome: Ediesse, 2002.

Mellen, Joan. *Filmguide to "The Battle of Algiers."* Bloomington: Indiana University Press, 1973.

Mereghetti, Paolo. *Il Mereghetti dizionario dei film 2000.* Milan: Baldini and Castoldi, 1999.

Michalczyk, John. "Franco Solinas: The Dialectic of Screenwriting." *Cineaste* 13, no. 2 (1984): 30–33.

———. *The Italian Political Filmmakers.* Rutherford, NJ: Farleigh Dickinson, 1986.

Micheli, Paola. *Il cinema di Blasetti, Parlò così.* Rome: Bulzoni Editore, 1990.

Microsoft Encarta Encyclopedia CD ROM, 1999.

Morgenstern, Joseph. "The Terrror." *Newsweek*, October 23, 1967, 102.

Moruzzi, Norma Claire. "Veiled Agents: Feminine Agency and Masquerade in *The Battle of Algiers.*" In *Negotiating at the Margins: The Gendered Discourses of Power and Resistance.* Ed. Sue Fisher and Kathy Davis. New Brunswick, NJ: Rutgers University Press, 1993.

Nichols, Bill. "Revolution and Melodrama: A Marxist View of Some Recent Films." *Cinema* (Los Angeles) 6, no. 1, 42–47.

Nirentein, Fiamma. *Gli antisemiti progressisti la forma nuova di un odio antico.* Milan: Rizzoli, 2004.

Pontecorvo, Gillo. *La Battaglia di Algeri.* DVD. Rome: DNC Home Entertainment, 2001.

———. *The Battle of Algiers.* DVD. Irvington, NY: Rialto Pictures, 2004.

———. "*The Battle of Algiers:* An Adventure in Filming." *American Cinematographer* (April 1967): 266–69.

———. *Un film di Gillo Pontecorvo: Queimada con Marlon Brando.* DVD. Rome: Eagle Pictures, 2003.

———. *Giovanna: Storia di un film e del suo restauro.* Ed. Antonio Medici. Rome: Ediesse, 2002.

———. *Kapò.* DVD. Rome: Cristaldi Film, 2003.

———. *Ogro.* DVD. Rome: Cristaldi Film, 2003.

———. *The Wide Blue Road.* DVD. Chatsworth, CA: Milestone Film and Video, 2003.

Porin, Pierre. "Le Cinema Algerien et *La Bataille d'Alger.*" *Positif* 79 (October 1966): 23–25.

Predal, Rene. *Fernando Solanas ou la rage de transformer le monde*. Paris: Telerama, 2001.

Racine, Robert W. *Bi-Weekly Newsletter of Mass Media Ministries*, December 11, 1967.

Rapf, Maurice. "High Drama in a History Restaged." *Life*, October 27, 1967.

Rivette, Jacques. "De l'abjection." *Les cahiers du cinema* 20, no. 120 (1961): 54–55.

Ryan, Paul. *Marlon Brando: A Portrait*. New York: Carrol and Graf, 1992.

Said, Edward. "The Dictatorship of Truth: An Interview with Gillo Pontecorvo." *Cineaste* 25, no. 2 (2000): 25.

———. *Gillo Pontecorvo: The Dictatorship of Truth*. Channel Four (Great Britain); Cinema Guild, 1992.

———. "The Quest for Gillo Pontecorvo." *Interview* 18, no. 11 (November 1988): 90–93.

Scott, A. O. "Third World Revolution as a Product of Italian Design." *New York Times*, September 19, 2004.

Scott, Janny. "A Palestinian Confronts Time: For Columbia Literary Critic, Cancer Is a Spur to Memory." *New York Times*, September 19, 1998.

Simon, John. "Fifth Festival: Growing Pains or Painful Growth?" *The New Leader*, October 9, 1967, 28. Reprinted in John Simon, *Movies into Film: Film Criticism, 1967–1970*. New York: Dial, 1971.

Solinas, Franco. *Gillo Pontecorvo's "The Battle of Algiers": A Film Written by Franco Solinas*. Ed. Pier Nico. New York: Scribner, 1973.

———. *Squarciò the Fisherman*. Trans. Frances Frenaye. New York: Dutton, 1958.

Solinas, Franco, G. Arlorio, and G. Pontecorvo. *Burn!: Story and Screenplay*. Los Angeles: United Artists/Combined Continuity, 1970.

Stam, Robert, and Ella Shohat. *Unthinking Eurocentrism: Multiculturalism and the Media*. New York: Routledge, 1994.

Stam, Robert, and Louise Spence. "Colonialism, Racism and Representation: An Introduction." In *Movies and Methods*, vol. 2, ed. Bill Nichols, 623–46. Berkley and Los Angeles: University of California Press, 1985.

Tassone, Aldo. *Parla il Cinema Italiano*. 1st vol. Paris: Edilig, 1982.

Thomas, Tony. *The Films of Marlon Brando*. Rev. ed. New York: Citadel Press Books, 1992.

Verdone, Luca. *I film di Alessandro Blasetti*. Rome: Gremese, 1989.

Vergano, Aldo. *Cronaca degli anni perduti: Memorie*. Firenze, Italy: Parenti, 1958.

Vincendeau, Ginette. *Pépé le Moko*. London: BFI, 1998.

Walsh, Moira. "*The Battle of Algiers*." *America*, November 4, 1967, 521–22.

Zavattini, Cesare. *Opere, 1931–1986*. Milan: Bompiani, 1991.

Index

About the Author

Carlo Celli is an associate professor at Bowling Green State University in Ohio. He has written extensively on Italian cinema and is the author of *The Divine Comic: The Cinema of Roberto Benigni* (Scarecrow, 2001).